# MY HALAL KITCHEN

# MY HALAL KITCHEN

GLOBAL RECIPES • COOKING TIPS • LIFESTYLE INSPIRATION

## YVONNE MAFFEI

**S**

**SURREY**
**BOOKS**

AN **AGATE** IMPRINT

CHICAGO

Printed in China

Photos on pages 40, 70, 73, 78, 85, 88, 91, 106, 113, 126, 132, 137, 148, 157, 158, 164, 174, 182, 190, and 192 by Peter McCullough
Photos on pages 65, 139, 147, 187, and 197 by Yvonne Maffei
Author photo on page 213 by Studio Miya Photography


Library of Congress Cataloging-in-Publication Data

Names: Maffei, Yvonne M., author.
Title: My halal kitchen : global recipes, cooking tips, and lifestyle
  inspiration / by Yvonne M. Maffei.
Description: Chicago : Surrey, an Agate imprint, 2016. | Includes
  bibliographical references and index.
Identifiers: LCCN 2016001808 (print) | LCCN 2016001999 (ebook) | ISBN
  9781572841741 (hardback) | ISBN 1572841745 (hardcover) | ISBN
  9781572847804 (ebook) | ISBN 1572847808 (ebook)
Subjects: LCSH: Islamic cooking. | Cooking, Middle Eastern. | Food--Religious
  aspects--Islam. | BISAC: COOKING / Regional & Ethnic / American / General.
  | COOKING / Regional & Ethnic / International. | COOKING / Methods /
  Baking. | SOCIAL SCIENCE / Islamic Studies. | LCGFT: Cookbooks.
Classification: LCC TX725.M628 M296 2016 (print) | LCC TX725.M628 (ebook) |
  DDC 641.5956--dc23
LC record available at http://lccn.loc.gov/2016001808


10 9 8 7 6 5 4 3 2 1                                             16 17 18 19 20

Surrey is an imprint of Agate Publishing.  Agate books are available in bulk at discount prices.

agatepublishing.com

*Bismillah ir Rahman ir Raheem.*
In the name of Allah (God),
the Most Compassionate,
the Most Merciful.

# Contents

# How to Use This Book

THANK YOU SO MUCH FOR CHOOSING THIS BOOK. In *My Halal Kitchen*, I aim to teach you how to cook an exciting variety of gloabl cuisine according to Islamic dietary guidelines—essentially, what is halal (permissible), regardless of the dish you are preparing. My intention is to demystify the concept of halal and show how easy it can be to prepare tasty dishes within this framework.

Rather than focusing on limitations, I offer a world of abundant culinary possibilities for you as a home cook. I will show you how easy and rewarding it is to use delicious alternatives to non-halal ingredients. You will see that halal is, in fact, a liberating way to cook, as there are more choices than ever before. I hope to inspire you to create halal meals at home by providing the tools, resources, and information you'll need.

My own need to source halal ingredients and create versions of the traditional dishes I grew up with led me to write a book from which I wanted to cook. The book also parallels my belief that the organic farm-to-table system is important to preserve and protect in our time. In fact, mainstream interest in health, wellness, clean eating, and locally grown and produced products has reached an all-time high, which is such a wonderful thing. Also, as Americans living in a multicultural society, we are much more willing to try dishes with roots in globally inspired cuisine. Those close to us are more likely to have traveled to faraway places or to have learned about different cultures, and subsequently can introduce us to new and exciting cuisines. Greater levels of consumer awareness have led to greater demand for transparency. We know far more today about the environmental impact of factory farming and treatment of agricultural laborers, which gives consumers the upper hand in supporting and demanding products be sourced from humanely treated animals and fair-trade conditions. In the context of halal, all of these concepts have traditionally held importance from a religious imperative and spiritual perspective.

As you'll learn in these pages, halal is not just about food: It plays a role in all matters of life and is considered a universal concept from which all of humanity can benefit. Every part of the farm-to-table cycle is significant, and transparency in the food cycle and holistic living are vital matters to Muslims, as a devout follower would never support inhumane treatment of animals or unjust treatment of workers just to purchase a cheaper product. All living creatures are taken into consideration and given their due respect.

You might have encountered this book because you or your loved ones are Muslim, or simply because you're interested in eating halal and care deeply about the origin of your food. I hope that people of all backgrounds will give my recipes a try, as halal is not just for Muslims—all you have to be is willing to learn more about it and give the delicious food a try.

I especially wanted to provide recipes that are more challenging to prepare while meeting halal dietary standards. For example, many desserts served in restaurants or ready-made in stores may contain alcohol and/or gelatin (which often contains pork by-products) and are not halal. Instead, I'll show you how to make these types of dishes the halal way.

Finding high-quality substitutes, as well as figuring out what sort of by-products are in certain food products, can be difficult for consumers. Fortunately, many of these substitutions are easy to make at home, and I'm eager to finally be able to share how to do that. As a result, I hope this book will make the way you shop and cook so much easier.

You'll find recipes derived from my own ethnic heritage and travels around the world. These dishes are meaningful to me because they are part of my life journey, and because they're homemade and halal, I feel good about sharing them.

During my childhood in Ohio, long before embracing a halal lifestyle, I developed a taste for Italian and Puerto Rican foods, as well as other ethnic cuisines. From my Sicilian father and grandmother, I inherited a love for Mediterranean food. Sunday dinners at my *nonna's* (grandmother's) house usually included homemade meatballs steeped in Nonna's marinara sauce, meaty lasagna, healthy salads, and gently steamed vegetables, like artichokes dipped in butter.

My mother is Puerto Rican, so meals with her side of the family were abundant with *arroz con frijoles* (rice and beans), *pasteles* wrapped in banana leaves, and sweet guava and coconut desserts, especially when my grandmother came to visit from the island. These experiences connect good food with the people I cherish most.

The gathering of family, friends, and neighbors is the perfect excuse to serve a homemade meal and something I'm incredibly passionate about doing for others. I think it's one of the kindest things we can do for the people in our lives. A great meal can neutralize negativity, drive conversations toward positive things, and reflect more of what everyone has in common than not.

Fast forward many years and many great food experiences where I found myself diving deep into the world of halal dietary guidelines. I discovered that I was in the middle of two worlds, needing to bridge a gap of understanding: On one side, non-Muslims had very little idea—except perhaps negative ones—of the concept of halal; and on the other side, the Muslim community lacked resources for halal products and recipe ideas that accommodated a growing interest in American and international fare. I felt an online presence was a space where I could provide just that.

In 2008, I started *MyHalalKitchen.com*, a halal food blog showcasing my culinary tips, halal recipes, and resources for finding quality halal food and wellness products. My goal for the blog—and also for this book—is to bridge the gap between the two worlds in which I live. My non-Muslim family and friends who don't eat halal are very curious about what halal means; the Muslim community of course embraces halal as a lifestyle, but many individuals long to try authentic Italian or Mexican dishes and are deterred because of the possibility that they contain pork or other non-halal ingredients. I decided my blog should inform both sides and show how easy it could be for everyone to join at the table and enjoy foods from a variety of cultures prepared according to halal standards.

To be clear, I am not a scholar of Islam by any means. I study food science and Islamic jurisprudence (*fiqh*) whenever I can—speaking to scholars, studying texts, listening to lectures, and attending courses—but I'm always and forever a student of these subjects. I'm sharing what I've learned and presenting the (sometimes debatable) facts I've gathered so you can decide for yourself how to cook and eat halal.

*My Halal Kitchen* has two primary sections: information and recipes. In the information section, you'll learn the meaning of halal in the context of food, how to source ingredients, which ingredients are most problematic, and what halal alternatives exist.

The heart of the book is the recipes section. In it, you'll not only find foundational recipes but also dishes traditionally made with alcohol or pork ingredients that are difficult to find in halal form. I think you'll find my recipes simple and easy to follow, and you'll have the comfort of knowing all of the ingredients are halal.

Combined, the information and recipe sections provide you with a comprehensive foundation of knowledge about halal foodways. I've provided you with the tools you'll need to make any recipe halal—for example, convenient charts that list substitutes for alcohol and pork. Many of the recipes also include variations for substitutes that can add entirely new flavors and twists from which you can create new dishes.

The inclusion of foundational foods like bread, pizza dough, and pie crust is to provide you with the ability to easily create recipes from scratch. You'll also find a vetted list of halal pantry products in the book's Resources section. When you're pinched for time, or just want to make things a little easier, you'll be able to improvise using commercially available products that I've hand-selected for their trusted sources and high quality.

## NOTE ON MEASUREMENTS

The recipes in this book were created, tested, and written using the United States customary system. Conversion charts for metric equivalencies are included in the back of the book.

# Glossary of Terms

In these pages, you'll find frequent references to ingredients commonly found in packaged foods that are incompatible with a halal diet, terms related to halal substitutes found in cooking and baking, and common vernacular relating to Islamic food practices and lifestyle. Here's a helpful glossary.

**Agar-Agar:** A naturally occurring jelly-like substance derived from algae, agar-agar is a suitable alternative to pork-based gelatins in many dishes. It has commonly been used in Asia for centuries to make jellies and candies, but can also be found throughout North America and Europe in powder or flake form.

**Ahadith:** See *Hadith.*

**Alhamdullilah (literally, "thank God"):** A phrase Muslims say, particularly after eating or drinking.

**Annatto:** Also known as *achiote* in Spanish, annatto is derived from the achiote tree. Its orange-reddish seeds are ground to add coloring to many Latin dishes and commercial food products.

**Bismillah (literally "in the name of God"):** A phrase Muslims say before starting an activity, including eating or drinking.

**Bone Char:** A product made by charring and grinding up animal bones (typically beef) that is used in the sugar industry to clarify sugar and give it a white color. Turbinado (raw cane sugar) and beet sugars definitely do *not* contain bone char, but it is important to note that all other refined sugars may or may not include bone char filtration as part of their processing.

**Citric Acid:** A preservative derived from citrus products that provides acidity in recipes or citrus flavoring to beverages.

***Dhabiha*:** The Islamic method of ritually slaughtering halal permissible animals for consumption; also written as *zabiha*.

**Eid (pronounced 'eed):** A celebration or feast.

**Eid ul Adha:** The Feast of the Sacrifice commemorates the willingness of Prophet Ibrahim (Abraham) to sacrifice his son, Ishmael, to God. Just as Ibrahim was about to perform the sacrifice, God intervened, and Ishmael was replaced with a ram. Muslims who can afford the involved cost to sacrifice an animal, such as a camel, cow, goat or sheep, and offer it as food for their families, neighbors, and the poor. This feast also marks the end of the Hajj season, a period of pilgrimage to Mecca, Saudi Arabia, that takes place annually. Most Muslims around the globe aim to participate in the Hajj at least once in their lifetime if they can afford it.

**Eid ul Fitr:** A feast or celebration marking the end of the holy month of Ramadan. During Ramadan, the faithful abstain from all food and drink from just before sunrise to sunset.

**Emulsifier:** A substance used to make an emulsion, or a mixture of two foods that ordinarily wouldn't blend well together, such as oil and water. Commercial emulsifiers are often used in foods like mayonnaise and ice cream to create a specific consistency. Homemade emulsions often involve adding ingredients in a specific order and then vigorously whisking them together, such as vinegar and oil combined to make a salad dressing.

**Enzyme:** A catalyst to a chemical reaction that helps foster changes in the chemical makeup of foods. They are most commonly used in cheesemaking, but enzymes also naturally occur in such fruits as papaya and pineapples. Commercial enzymes can be derived from animal, vegetable, or microbial sources.

***Fiqh*:** Islamic jurisprudence, which means the science, study, and theory of law.

**Flavor Extract:** The result of a process whereby a substance is contained in a solvent, such as water, alcohol, or something else that will extract its flavor.

**Gelatin:** A substance obtained from the collagen of particular animals (most commonly pigs and cows). Gelatin is a protein extracted via boiling the animal's connective tissues, bones, and skin in water. The result is a flexible, odorless, colorless gel that is both water soluble and edible, making it a useful ingredient for jellies, cakes, and commercial products that must remain firm and stable during their shelf life. It is also used as a clarifying agent in drinks, such as apple juice.

**Glycerin (Glycerol):** A product obtained by saponifying fats and oils that is used to sweeten and preserve foods. It is also a solvent used in skincare and medicinal products due to its syrup-like consistency and sweet yet colorless and odorless characteristics.

**Genetically Modified Organism (GMO):** An organism whose genetic makeup has been altered using genetic engineering methods and techniques.

***Hadith* (pl. *Ahadith*):** The narrations attributed to the Companions of Prophet Muhammed ﷺ, about the Prophet Muhammed ﷺ, also known as the recorded sayings of Prophet Muhammed ﷺ.

**Halal:** An Arabic term meaning *permissible* that addresses everything from food to finance to dress, as well as actions and interactions among people in society. Muslims believe that what is prescribed in the Qur'an as halal is the word of Allah (God) and thus must be obeyed and perceived as good for all, rather than as limiting or restrictive without benefit.

**Halal Certification Body:** An organization that certifies products and their processing methodologies as halal. The organization combines the efforts of food scientists and scholars who understand modern food industry practices as well as Islamic theology and its various interpretations with regard to what deems a food product as halal.

**Haram:** The opposite of halal—*impermissible*. The term is used regarding topics from food to finance to dress and about actions and interactions among people in society.

***Iftar:*** A meal that breaks a day of fasting. The term is most commonly used during the month of Ramadan but can be used to mean breaking a fast throughout the year.

**Islam:** A religion focused on voluntary submission to Allah (God); the monotheistic faith is practiced by more than two billion people spanning all manner of ethnic origin and socio-economic status.

**Istihalah:** The process by which something impure becomes pure.

**L-Cysteine:** Often labeled as a dough conditioner or softener, this product is commercially used as an additive in bread products, including pizza dough, ready-made breads, and rolls. Its purpose is to make the doughs more pliable or easier to form. It is made from such substances as hog hair, human hair, and duck feathers. The most common source for L-cysteine is hog hair from China, although much of the L-cysteine made of human hair and duck feathers comes from India.

**Madhhab:** A school of thought in Islamic jurisprudence (*fiqh*). There are four major schools, each named after their founders: Imam Shafi'i, Imam Ahmad ibn Hanbal, Imam Malik, and Imam Abu Hanifa.

**Makrooh:** An Arabic word used in an Islamic context to describe something disliked but not haram.

**Mashbooh:** An Arabic word in an Islamic context to describe something vague or very doubtful.

**Mono and diglycerides:** Synthetic fats produced from glycerol and fatty acids that are used as additives and emulsifiers in food products. Mono and diglycerides can originate from plants or animals.

**Muslim:** One who believes in and follows the five pillars of Islam: 1) Believes in one God, Allah, and the Last Day; 2) Believes in the last Messenger, Prophet Muhammed ﷺ; 3) Observes the daylight-hour fast during the month of Ramadan if he or she is healthy enough; 4) Pays the *zakat* (money given to charity each year); and 5) Makes the Hajj (pilgrimage to Mecca) at least once in a lifetime if he or she is capable of doing so.

**Organic (Food):** A food that is produced and harvested using organic agricultural methods and free of pesticides and chemically sourced fertilizers.

**Pectin:** A plant-derived gelatinous substance used to make jams, jellies, and other fruit preserves that typically is made from apples or citrus fruits. It should not be confused with animal-sourced gelatin or agar-agar.

**Prophet Muhammed** 🕌**:** The man believed by Muslims to be the last Messenger and Prophet of God to all of mankind. Muhammed is believed to be the last of a long line of prophets, beginning with Adam. The Arabic inscription 🕌 is often written after his and other prophets' names to indicate the phrase "peace be upon him."

**Qur'an:** Sometimes referred to as the Koran, this holy book of guidance for Muslims is believed to have been revealed through the Angel Jibreel (Gabriel) to the Prophet Muhammed 🕌 in stages over a span of 23 years.

**Ramadan:** The ninth month in the lunar-based Islamic calendar is a holy month of fasting. During Ramadan, all believers healthy enough to fast refrain from intimate relations with a spouse or consuming food and water from just before sunrise until sunset each day. The fast is broken at different times around the world, according to the believer's geographic location.

**Rennet:** An enzyme found in the stomachs of young mammals that allows them to process their mothers' milk. This natural enzyme also helps to coagulate, or thicken, milk when making cheese.

**Shari'a:** Islamic law or theology derived primarily from the Qur'an and *Ahadith*.

**Suhoor:** The meal consumed just before the fasting day begins. The term is typically used in reference to the month of Ramadan.

**Sunnah:** Religious practices established by the Prophet Muhammed 🕌 that incorporate both his sayings and his traditions.

**Tayyib:** An Arabic word meaning *good* and *pure*. In reference to food, its meaning indicates that the food is natural, unaltered, and uncorrupted.

**Vanilla Essence:** A synthetic form of vanilla extract.

**Vanilla Powder:** A powder made from ground vanilla beans. It can be a synthetic product or a natural product mixed with sugar or other sweeteners, so be sure to carefully read the label if using.

**Vanillin:** An artificial or synthetic version of vanilla extract typically made from wood pulp.

# Overview of Halal Food and Cooking

# CHAPTER 1

# Halal Foods 101

IF YOU ARE COOKING HALAL, you are cooking without the use of haram (impermissible) ingredients, per Islamic dietary guidelines. Embracing halal and avoiding the haram is an act of worship for Muslims.

In the Qur'an, Allah (God) says, "Eat of the *Tayyibāt* [all kinds of halal (legal) foods] which Allah has made lawful [meat of slaughtered halal animals, milk products, fats, vegetables, fruits, etc.] and do righteous deeds" (Surah Al Mu'minun [23:51]).

The four *madhabib*, or schools of thought regarding Islamic jurisprudence, have some differences of opinion regarding meat, seafood, and by-products of certain foods. I'll elaborate on those in the next chapter, but in brief, you'll find that halal options are much more abundant than they are restrictive. Halal animals and foods include:

- Land animals such as buffalo, camels, cows, deer, elk, goats, horses, sheep, wild donkeys, and zebras; poultry, including chickens, doves, ducks, geese, pheasants, pigeons, quail, sparrows, and turkey; and small game, such as rabbits
- Non-predatory animals without fangs or claws (wild or domestic)

- All water creatures, including fish, mollusks, shellfish, and crustaceans (Note: Fish and locusts need not be ritually slaughtered.)
- Any animal that is to be slaughtered as halal must have been fed a proper diet and must be healthy. This extends to ensuring that the animal has not consumed other animal parts.
- Any plants and liquids that are neither poisonous nor intoxicating are also halal.

Muslims believe that halal foods benefit humankind and that haram foods pose a risk of harm to one's body and to society as well. Some haram animals and foods include:

- Pork and any flesh of swine, as well as pork by-products
- Domesticated donkeys and mules
- Predatory animals, including those with fangs and claws
- Some amphibians
- Carrion (i.e., roadkill or any other animal that died in an unknown way)
- Wine and intoxicants
- Any substances that intoxicate or harm the body, or any substances that cause more harm than benefit to the body (i.e., drugs, cigarettes, etc.)
- Any animals killed in a violent way (i.e., gored, attacked by wild animals, beaten or clubbed, etc.)
- Any permitted animals that were not ritually slaughtered, except for fish and locusts
- Human body parts or by-products of the body (i.e., placenta, urine, and feces)
- Any animal dedicated or devoted to other than Allah (God)

## RULES FOR HALAL SLAUGHTER

All meat deemed halal should also be slaughtered in accordance with the Islamic method, which is known as *dhabiha*. For the slaughter to be in line with halal, the person performing the slaughter must be a sane adult, and he or she must be Christian, Jewish, or Muslim. An exception is made for animals destined to be consumed during Eid ul Adha, the Festival of the Sacrifice of Abraham; these animals must be slaughtered by a Muslim.

Requirements for ritual slaughter include:

- The name of God (Allah) should be mentioned at the time of slaughter: "*Bismillah, Allahu Akbar*" ("In the name of God, God is the greatest")
- The animal should be alive, healthy, and conscious at the time of slaughter
- Slaughter should be done with one swift cut of a sharp knife
- The windpipe, esophagus, and two jugular veins must be cut; the head should not be cut off, nor should the knife penetrate the spinal cord
- Slaughter must not be performed where non-halal animals, such as pigs, are being slaughtered or processed

Additional desirable practices include:

- The knife should be concealed from the animal going to slaughter, so it is not frightened
- Water should be given to the animal, and it should be calm
- The slaughter should be performed out of the sight of other live animals
- All precautions should be taken to prevent unnecessary suffering

# CHAPTER 2

# Problematic Ingredients for Halal Consumers

W E LIVE IN A COMPLEX WORLD, resulting in food processing that bears little resemblance to methods used in the past. Traditional staples, like bread or yogurt, are not made at home using a few simple ingredients. Instead, they are commercially produced with countless additives and preservatives.

Some companies have made significant efforts to produce all-natural or organic foods, which is commendable, but not all are halal. It's daunting to deconstruct food labels in order to understand the origin of each ingredient, but it's worthwhile to do so. I'm all for getting back to the basics, in terms of the food we eat. I advocate that we put our money to work for us by shopping wisely and demanding real change and transparency in the way food is produced. In return for the effort, I believe we'll consume better quality food; we'll help eliminate harmful chemicals, hormones, and fertilizers from the environment; we'll protect the bees, which are vital pollinators; and we'll help ensure equal access to quality organic foods, making them the norm once again. This food revolution is occurring in the culinary world right here, right now, and I find it fascinating that these ideas have always been the heart of the Islamic concept of halal and *tayyib* (permissible and pure). Islam is rooted in the belief that human beings are stewards of the earth. With that privilege comes accountability—a responsibility to protect and care for the earth, and for all its creatures.

Changes in shopping and consumption habits will take time and organized effort. In the meantime, it's useful to know as much as possible about the foods you do purchase and consume. As a result, you'll be very surprised to find out the origin of some ingredients.

It should be noted that the four *madhabib* differ on whether certain food products are halal, doubtful, discouraged, or outright haram because some ingredients undergo chemical changes during their creation. For example, some say that if an ingredient that is originally haram (wine, an intoxicant) goes through a chemical change that renders it halal (vinegar, which is not an intoxicant), then the final product is halal. Others disagree.

Some scholars have addressed the perceived hardship of eating halal in such a complex food world. They argue against making things harder than they need to be, as the purpose of the Shari'a is to make life easier. They say that since following the halal and avoiding the haram is an act of worship, convenience in food sources should make that worship easier to do. I would also add that other issues integral to food production and vital to following the teachings of Islam should be addressed, as many halal consumers have concerns and questions over things such as social justice/ethical consumerism, as well as the highly debatable issues surrounding biotechnology in the form of genetically engineered foods, or GMOs, and how those affect the health and safety of both humans and livestock.

At the end of the day, the most consumers can do is learn the origins of a product's ingredients, know the halal options, and make informed decisions from there.

# Problematic Food Products and Ingredients

**Alcohol:** Different types of alcohol are used in food production, and not all are intoxicants. Sugar alcohols, for example, are chemically the same as other types of alcohol, but they do not intoxicate. Used as sweeteners in processed foods, they go by several different names, including xylitol, sorbitol, and mannitol. According to the Islamic Food and Nutrition Council of America (IFANCA), alcohol may be used as a solvent in flavorings, but it must be reduced to below 0.5% to receive a halal certification.

**Breads and Doughs:** The dough conditioner L-cysteine is often added to soften these products. Sources could include human hair, hog hair, and duck feathers.

**Hard or Soft Cheeses:** Cheeses are often made using animal rennet, which is a naturally occurring enzyme present in animal stomachs. It is, of course, likely that an animal

## WHAT IS RENNET, AND WHERE DOES IT COME FROM?

Rennet is a natural enzyme found in the stomachs of young mammals. It allows them to process their mothers' milk. This enzyme also helps to coagulate, or thicken, milk when making cheese. Its key component is a protease enzyme called chymosin, or rennin, and it also contains the enzymes lipase and pepsin.

Rennet is used in cheesemaking to speed up the coagulation process in the separation of curds and whey after a starter culture is added to milk. The most common sources of rennet for cheesemaking are:

- Animal (typically a young calf, goat or sheep)
- Vegetable (from plants like nettles or thistle)
- Microbial (from fungi and yeast)
- Genetically modified sources
- Other coagulants used in cheesemaking, including acids like vinegar and lemon juice. These are commonly used to make ricotta or paneer cheeses.

Today, microbial rennet is commonly found in cheese products. It is suitable for vegetarians and also is halal.

from which rennet was obtained was not slaughtered in accordance with Islamic practices. Other enzymes used to make cheese could also be an issue if they originate from non-halal animals or those not slaughtered in accordance with Islamic guidelines. Additionally, the rinds of some cheeses are made with lard or wine.

## WHAT IS VINEGAR?

The word *vinegar* literally translates from the French to "sour wine." It is basically alcohol that has undergone a chemical souring process (fermentation) and reached a point where it is no longer alcoholic in nature, but is instead acetic acid, which is why acidity levels are typically listed on bottles of vinegar. Vinegar can be derived from a number of substances but most commonly originates from grapes (wine), apples (hard cider), or corn or wheat (grain alcohol).

### How Vinegar Is Made

As just mentioned, vinegar is the result of a chemical change process that renders the final product free of alcohol. In the Islamic sciences, this is an example of *istihala*. Balsamic vinegars often list wine as an ingredient. That's because balsamic vinegar is made from late-harvest grape must—whole, pressed grapes that have been cooked, concentrated, and aged for a number of years. Often, a manufacturer will list wine as an ingredient in balsamic vinegar for one of two reasons: a) because the grapes were aged and turned to wine in order to make the vinegar; or b) because wine was added after the vinegar was made, to add more flavor (which is rare but could happen).

From my understanding and study of this process, the only way that alcohol would remain in the final vinegar product is if the second scenario occurs, and the alcohol is added after the vinegar is made. I contacted many balsamic vinegar manufacturers, both gourmet and not, and not one indicated that wine was added to the end of the vinegar-making process. If a product is labeled as vinegar, it has been tested and its acidity levels have been proven. Carefully investigate each brand to ensure you are comfortable with the end product.

**Chocolate Liquor:** A liquid paste produced when cocoa beans are roasted and ground, it is the basis of all chocolate products. It does not contain any alcohol.

**Dairy:** Check labels for Vitamin D3, which is a pork-derived vitamin supplement.

**Emulsifiers:** These may be derived from bovine or porcine sources; they are commonly used in whipping cream, mayonnaise, confections, peanut butter, and ice cream.

**Gelatin:** Pork is an inexpensive source of gelatin, which is often found in yogurt and juices.

**Vanilla Products:** Vanilla extract, vanillin, vanilla powder, or other vanilla flavoring substances could be a concern to those who wish to avoid even small amounts of alcohol.

**Vinegar:** Check with producers about the addition of alcohol to final vinegar products.

**Whey:** A by-product of cheesemaking, whey is the liquid part of milk that separates from the curds when making cheese.

# Problematic Ingredients When Eating Out

ASIAN RESTAURANTS

*Shin mirin* is a Japanese cooking wine often added to teriyaki sauce. *Sake*, another type of Japanese alcohol, is also sometimes in Asian sauces. There are teriyaki sauces made without alcohol, so just ask. Common terms for Japanese alcoholic beverages include *sake*, *shin mirin*, and *shōchū*.

Naturally brewed **soy sauce** often contains alcohol, but soy sauces that contain acidified hydrolyzed soy protein generally do not. Check labels and call the manufacturer, if necessary, to be sure. Chinese soy sauce is called *jiangyou* or *chiyou*, and Korean soy sauce is called *josean ganjang*. Philippine soy sauce is called *toyo* and fish sauces from there are often referred to as *patis*. Vietnamese soy sauce is called *xi-dau*.

Many, but not all, **fish sauces** are also fermented and contain alcohol. *Kecap* is an Indonesian term for all fermented sauces, including fish sauces. The same term is also widely used in Malaysia to indicate a type of soy or fish sauce.

The word for pig in Japanese is *buta*, so you can look for it on menus or ask whether it's included in a certain recipe.

If you don't eat shellfish or fish without scales, you may want to avoid sushi with the following types of fish: abalone (*awabi*), clams (*hamaguri*), baby neck clams (*asari*), crab (*kani*), cuttlefish (*kou-ika*), jellyfish (*kurage*), spiny lobster (*ise-ebi*), mussel (*i-gai*), octopus (*tako*), oyster (*kaki*), scallops (*hotate gai*), sea cucumber (*namako*), sea urchin (*uni*), squid (*aori-ika*), and shrimp (*odori*).

If you are particular about eating eel, note that anything that starts with *una*, such as *unagi*, indicates that the dish contains eel.

### FISH AND SEAFOOD RESTAURANTS

At many fine restaurants, seafood dishes are often prepared with some type of wine. In the southern states, fish and seafood are often breaded and deep-fried in oil. At one time, lard (pork fat) was the usual frying fat in the South, but it's uncommon today. Always ask to be sure.

When fish is breaded and fried, not only should you ask what type of oil it is fried in but also whether other foods (perhaps a pork product) are also fried in the same baskets and oil baths. Also ask if the batter is a beer batter, which is quite common in Southern dishes.

Most fish dipping sauces tend to be mayonnaise-based (tartar sauce) or ketchup-based (cocktail sauce). If a sauce contains mustard, be aware that some mustards contains wine (e.g., Dijon). Be sure to check labels on packets or bottles or ask your server for a list of ingredients.

Anything listed on a menu as a fish fillet or *filete* (Spanish) is almost always a fish with scales, like tilapia. If you don't eat shellfish or fish without scales, you may want to avoid ordering the types of seafood listed in the preceding section on Asian restaurants. You can also refer to the information in the previous section on Asian restaurants regarding fish sauces.

## ITALIAN RESTAURANTS

At Italian restaurants, a vinegar might be labeled as "wine vinegar," but that does not mean it actually contains wine; in fact, most do not.

Be mindful of seafood dishes, as many are cooked in wine. Because sauces are often made ahead of time, the restaurant may not be able to serve a fish entrée without wine, so be sure to ask.

*Peperoni* in Italian does not refer to the pepperoni sausage that's so popular on pizzas in the United States; in Italian, the word means "pepper," as in the vegetable.

Pork-based gelatin may be used in such dishes as tiramisù; lard (pig fat) may be used when baking cannoli shells to make them extra crispy.

Italian sausages are generally made with a mixture of pork and beef or pork and veal.

Italian words for alcoholic beverages include *rum, amaretto* (not to be confused with *amarena* cherries), *vodka, limoncello,* and *vino* (wine). Italian words for different types of pork include *mortadella, prosciutto, salami, pancetta,* and *lardo.*

Be sure to ask about all the components of your dessert before ordering. For example, sometimes the cherries served atop *spumoni* ice cream have been soaked in rum or amaretto. Italian pastries, such as tiramisù, are sometimes prepared with liquor as flavoring. Some types include brandy, rum, and amaretto.

Like Italian restaurants, French restaurants often cook their meats and fish in wine. French pastries often contain wine or other types of alcohol, such as vermouth or Calvados (apple brandy liqueur), to flavor everything from ice creams and sorbets to mousses, crèmes, and tarts. If you encounter a dessert with chocolate liquor, rest assured that it does not contain alcohol; rather, it is a combination of cocoa solids and cocoa butter.

When scanning a menu at a French restaurant, look for French terms for meat, including *bifteck* (beefsteak), *boeuf* (beef), *porc* (pork), and *charcuterie* (literally means "cooked meat"). *Charcuterie* could refer to any type of beef, lamb, or pork.

French words for various forms of alcohol include *bière* (beer), Calvados (apple brandy), and *vin* (wine).

## MEDITERRANEAN (GREEK, SPANISH, ETC.) RESTAURANTS

The Mediterranean Sea is bordered by a huge variety of nations. Thus "Mediterranean cuisine" includes a diverse range of foods, including those of France, Italy, Spain, Greece, and Turkey, and the islands of Cyprus, Malta, Sardinia, and Sicily. In these regions, just about every type of meat and fish are consumed—and so is alcohol, especially in cooking. When a restaurant describes itself as serving "Mediterranean cuisine," chances are that you'll find the food to be a combination of the countries and regions listed above. Some things to be aware of are:

Baked goods are sometimes prepared using such liquors as brandy, rum, and amaretto, as mentioned in the previous section.

After-dinner drinks described as palate cleansers or *aperitifs* are often alcoholic drinks. One example is *limoncello* (an Italian drink that is a mix of lemon zest, alcohol, and sugar water); another is *ouzo*, an anise-flavored Greek alcoholic beverage.

Many Spanish appetizers, known as tapas, could be topped with or wrapped in pork products like *jamón* or *chorizo*.

Sauces in pasta and rice are more often than not prepared using wine or vodka as part of the base, especially in seafood entrées. Don't assume the alcohol to be part of the dish description in the menu; ask your waiter instead and if he/she seems unsure, ask to confirm with the chef who prepared the dish.

Spanish terms for pork include *jamón, chorizo, prosciutto, salami, pancetta,* and *cochinillo* (baby suckling pig).

## MEXICAN RESTAURANTS

With Mexican restaurants being so popular, it's a shame to avoid them on the assumption that everything is made with pork. It simply isn't true, and more and more Mexican restaurants are using vegetable oils to cook dishes that accommodate the needs of their vegan and vegetarian customers, which is also good for halal consumers. *Manteca* is the Spanish word for lard or pork fat. Traditionally, many Mexican items such as *frijoles* (beans) were fried in it.

Spanish words for pork include *puerco, cerdo, chicharron, manteca, jamón, chorizo,* and *carnitas,* which is a popular Mexican dish of roasted, grilled, or braised pork.

Spanish words for alcohol include *cerveza* (beer), *margarita, vino* (wine), and *tequila.*

## ICE CREAM SHOPS

In general, ice cream parlors in the United States don't serve many flavors with alcohol, but there are some things to keep in mind. It should be noted that scholars debate whether or not something with gelatin is halal based on the concept of *istihalah.*

Marshmallow, which is usually made from pork-derived gelatin, may find its way into some flavors—rocky road, for example, commonly has marshmallow. Whenever you see white swirls in a flavor, be sure to ask, as it could be marshmallow.

Bubble gum–flavored ice cream, which is sometimes called "rainbow," may contain a pork-based product also found in gum.

Rum is the most common alcoholic addition to American ice cream. It's often paired with cherry or vanilla ice cream.

# CHAPTER 3

# Halal Ingredient Substitutes

DOES ALCOHOL REALLY BURN OFF DURING COOKING? This is commonly asked by people who inquire for religious reasons or simply avoid alcohol for health reasons or personal preferences. In fact, US Department of Agriculture data indicates that alcohol does *not* burn off completely during cooking, even over significantly long periods of time. It may burn off somewhat, but scholars from all four of the *madhahib* agree that *khamr* (wine) or alcohol used for cooking will render a dish haram.

I've researched and tested a variety of alcohol substitutes for use in both cooking and baking by detecting the origins of the alcohol flavors and figuring out a halal alternative. For example, since Calvados comes from apples, apple juice is a great substitute. The different types of grapes used to make the wine I'm replacing determines the type of grape juice I'll use in a dish.

This section provides handy charts for alcohol burn-off rates and alcohol substitutes for your reference. Use the same amount of the substitute as you would for the alcohol itself.

## Alcohol Burn-off Chart (US Department of Agriculture)

| PREPARATION METHOD | % RETAINED |
|---|---|
| Alcohol added to boiling liquid and removed from heat | 85% |
| Alcohol flamed | 75% |
| No heat, stored overnight | 70% |
| Baked, 25 minutes, alcohol not stirred into mixture | 45% |
| *Baked/simmered dishes with alcohol stirred into mixture:* | |
| 15 minutes cooking time | 40% |
| 30 minutes cooking time | 35% |
| 1 hour cooking time | 25% |
| 1½ hours cooking time | 20% |
| 2 hours cooking time | 10% |
| 2½ hours cooking time | 5% |

*Source: US Department of Agriculture*

## Alcoholic Beverages

| INSTEAD OF THIS | USE THIS |
|---|---|
| **Beer** | White grape juice or apple juice |
| **Brandy** | Peach purée or peach juice |
| **Calvados** | Apple juice (not from concentrate) |
| **Champagne** | Sparkling apple juice, sparkling grape juice, sparkling fruit-flavored juice, plain sparkling water, club soda, or ginger ale |
| **Red wine** | High-quality grape juice, with no sugar added |
| **Rum** | Blackstrap molasses and raw cane sugar mixed with water (equal parts each) |
| **Sambuca** | Anise-flavored Italian syrup |
| **Vodka** | White grape juice, with a squeeze of fresh lemon juice |

## Extracts and Flavorings

| INSTEAD OF THIS | USE THIS |
| --- | --- |
| Almond extract | Almond bakery emulsion |
| Amaretto | Peach purée or peach juice |
| Aniseed extract | Pure aniseed oil |
| Lemon extract | Lemon oil or lemon bakery emulsion |
| Orange extract | Orange oil or orange bakery emulsion |
| Rum | Blackstrap molasses and raw cane sugar mixed with water (equal parts each) |

# Pork Substitutes

Pork and its many by-products are in a surprising number of consumable products in the modern food world. Thus, it's important for the halal consumer to know how to create dishes with appropriate halal substitutes. Use the same amount of the substitute as you would for the pork itself.

| INSTEAD OF THIS | USE THIS |
| --- | --- |
| Bacon, *lardons* | Beef breakfast strips |
| Pork chorizo | Beef chorizo, sejouk/sujuk (Turkish-style beef sausage), *merguez* |
| Gelatin (from pork) | Beef gelatin, agar-agar (also known as fish flakes or sea algae flakes) |
| Ham | Roasted or smoked turkey breast |
| Lard | Chicken fat, duck fat |
| Mortadella | Beef mortadella |
| Pancetta | Smoked turkey strips |
| Prosciutto | Duck prosciutto |
| Salami | Beef salami, turkey salami |

# CHAPTER 4

# Creating a Halal Kitchen Pantry

I T CAN BE DAUNTING to figure out whether each food item you pick up is halal and healthy, but you are your best advocate when it comes to having easy access to these types of halal products. More than ever before, many products are free of the usual haram suspects, but some products deemed halal contain chemicals, artificial dyes, sweeteners, and other synthetic elements I don't want to consume. As a Muslim, I have an obligation to care for the body my Creator gave me by feeding it nutritious and healthy food that is free of impurities.

In North America, it's a lot easier than it was 10 years ago—or even 5 years ago—to find quality halal foods containing healthy ingredients and offering transparency in their contents, as more and more products enter the market to fill the demand. That's a great thing. These products tout not only health-consciousness, but also convenience for the consumer, a sometimes difficult combination to produce. I choose products with the fewest ingredients, and those with the most natural ones possible. That way I know what I'm

getting, and it's so much easier to determine if it's halal when it's not specifi-
cally labeled as such. Below is a short checklist that can help you ensure what
you bring home is truly halal.

## TIPS FOR BUYING HALAL

- Get to know the owner of any store where you buy meat.* Ask where the meat comes from, how it has been raised (i.e., fed and treated), and about the slaughtering process. If there isn't a visible certification somewhere in the store or if the owner is unwilling to discuss the meat's halal status, take it as a sign that transparency isn't the store's normal policy.
- Join a community-sponsored agriculture (CSA) group. Few, if any, offer halal meat as part of the CSA, but you can always get milk, cheese, and organic produce. It's also a great way to get to know the food producers and other like-minded individuals in your community.
- When buying artisanal cheeses, ask if the rinds are washed with wine or lard.
- Know the halal certification agencies, the types of products they verify, and their reputation in the community and/or country in which they operate.
- Grow your own food, even if it's just a few things. It makes you aware of what it takes to get food to your plate and provides a deeper appreciation for the simplicity of all-natural ingredients. Besides, it's easier to cook and eat halal with healthy homegrown ingredients.
- When shopping, buy all-natural, pesticide-free food products.
- Study the Sunnah foods, those that the Prophet Muhammed ﷺ ate. It was the practice of Prophet Muhammed ﷺ to eat nutrient-dense foods, and he ate everything in moderation. See the Resources section on p. 200.
- Get familiar with the brands of quality halal products and where to find them (see the Resources section on p. 200).
- If you can't find an alcohol-free vanilla, peppermint, or lemon extract for baking, substitute real vanilla bean, fresh crushed mint leaves, or lemon zest. Or make your own—see my recipes for extracts on pp. 53–56.

* Halal meat stores almost always carry other halal-certified ingredients, but you can find many in your local supermarket. Check the Islamic Food and Nutrition Council of America's (IFANCA) website, ifanca.org, for a list of products. Formulas change often, so be sure to check when it was last updated.

# Setting Up a Halal Kitchen

A halal kitchen needs no particular type of appliance or utensil. However, where halal and non-halal ingredients exist in the same area, care does need to be taken so that cross-contamination of ingredients doesn't occur. There doesn't need to be an entirely separate kitchen to prepare halal meals, but storage and cooking areas should be kept separate at all times. As long as halal foods are not mixed with and don't touch other foods (e.g., potatoes cooked in lard or beef fat from non-halal sources), and utensils are not shared between halal and haram ingredients, a dish prepared in that kitchen would be considered halal. Cooking in separate pots and using separate utensils that have been thoroughly cleaned, especially between uses with questionable ingredients, is also a must.

For your home, here are some must-have staples:

- Alcohol-free flavored extracts
- Real vanilla beans
- All-natural fruit juices, for cooking and baking when wine is called for in a recipe (i.e., grape, white grape, cherry, pineapple, or apple)*
- Animal and vegetable broths, to add more depth of flavor to dishes
- Food-grade glycerin, to make your own extracts
- Agar-agar, a non-animal gelatin source, to make molds and jellies

  * I usually purchase them in the small juice box size for use in recipes.

# Recipes

CHAPTER 5

# Broths

BROTHS, ALSO KNOWN AS *stocks* (British), *brodos* (Italian), and *bouillons* (French), have been used in societies all around the world for centuries. They're quite simple—animal bones boiled in water for a lengthy amount of time. They are integral to most soups and stews, and in many cultures, they are even served alone to help restore health to the sick because they provide the body with essential vitamins and minerals like calcium and magnesium. In supermarkets today, much of the packaged meat is boneless, and many commercial broths are loaded with salt, with the exception of a few (see the Resources section on p. 200). We've drifted away from the old ways, from making our own broths at home.

Broths made from animal bones contain important minerals, such as calcium, magnesium, phosphorous, silicon, and sulfur—all of which are easy for us to absorb. A little vinegar added to the pot helps extract the calcium from the bones, enriching the benefits of the broth. The resulting gelatin in broth helps contribute to the healthy growth of hair and nails. Just about every culture has a classic pick-me-up broth recipe that includes some sort of soup or similar dish made using the broth of animal bones.

I believe that broths are an incredibly important part of healthy cooking, and when it comes to adding real, all-natural flavor to your food, there really is no substitute for them. Professional chefs and high-end restaurants take the time to make their own because they know it is the essence and foundation of great cooking—even a purely vegetable-based broth will add really rich flavor to dishes that would otherwise result in a mediocre to bland taste. As a home cook, I know my dishes would also lack the depth of flavor if I didn't use broth when cooking. In my opinion, and to the best of my knowledge, there is only one high-quality halal broth on the market (see the Resources section on p. 200), so it's worth the effort to learn to make broth yourself so you have extra on hand when needed. If you set aside a little bit of time to collect lamb, beef, and chicken bones from your butcher, you can easily make and freeze large batches of the different types of broths. They're super easy to defrost and use in soups and stews or to help bring someone you love back to good health with a bowl of it all on its own. Freeze them in containers and/or in ice-cube trays for those times when you only need a small amount for a recipe. It doesn't take much to be your family's own gourmet home cook, and making broth at home is a great way to shine.

**IN THIS CHAPTER**

# Beef Broth

*Beef broth adds incredibly rich flavor to soups, stews, and even roasts. Keep your fridge or freezer stocked with it to quickly and easily enhance meals.*

2–4 tablespoons olive oil

5 pounds beef bones, including some meat and marrow (can be a variety of bones)

1 gallon water

3 carrots, roughly chopped

2 onions, roughly chopped

1½ cups chopped tomatoes

2 stalks celery, roughly chopped

3 cloves garlic, peeled

⅓ cup white balsamic vinegar

¼ cup tomato paste

Assortment of fresh or dried herbs and spices (optional)

1  In a large stockpot over medium–low heat, gently heat the oil. Add the beef bones and sauté for 2 to 3 minutes, until the bones and any meat are slightly browned. Remove from the heat.

2  Remove the bones from the stockpot and rinse them well. Clean the pot and return the bones to it. Add the water and return it to medium–high heat. Bring to a boil.

3  Reduce the heat to medium–low. Simmer, uncovered, for 1½ hours, skimming off any film that rises to the surface at 15- to 20-minute intervals.

4  Add the carrots, onions, tomatoes, celery, garlic, and vinegar to the stockpot and stir in the tomato paste. Add the fresh or dried herbs and spices, if using. Raise the heat to medium–high and bring to a boil.

5  Reduce the heat to medium–low. Simmer, uncovered, for 4 hours, skimming off any film that rises to the surface at 15- to 20-minute intervals. Remove from the heat and set aside to cool to room temperature.

6  Using a fine sieve, strain out any food solids, herbs, and spices.

7  Store in a tightly sealed, food-safe glass container. Store in the refrigerator for 1 week or in the freezer for a few months. Before using, be sure to skim any accumulated fat from the surface.

# Chicken Broth

*Chicken broth is the most versatile of all broths because it goes so well with both vegetable and chicken dishes. Use it to flavor rice, soups, and to moisten a chicken roasting in the oven.*

2–4 tablespoons olive oil

1 whole chicken or the bones of 1 chicken with some meat

2½ quarts water

1 pound mushrooms, chopped

2 carrots, roughly chopped

1 onion, roughly chopped

2 stalks celery, roughly chopped

5 cloves garlic

1 cup chopped fresh curly or flat leaf parsley leaves and stems

1 teaspoon dried or 2 sprigs fresh thyme

3 bay leaves

¼ cup white balsamic vinegar or white distilled vinegar

1  In a large stockpot over medium–low heat, gently heat the oil. Add the chicken or bones and sauté for 5 minutes. Remove from the heat.

2  Add the water and the vegetables to the pot and return it to medium–high heat. Bring to a boil.

3  Reduce the heat to medium–low and add the herbs and vinegar. Simmer, uncovered, for 4 to 6 hours, skimming off any film that rises to the surface at 15- to 20-minute intervals. Remove from the heat and set aside to cool to room temperature.

4  Using a fine sieve, strain out and discard any food solids, herbs, and spices.

5  Store in a tightly sealed, food-safe glass container. Store in the refrigerator for 1 week or in the freezer for a few months. Before using, be sure to skim any accumulated fat from the surface.

# Lamb Broth

*If you make a lot of dishes with lamb, this is a must-have broth to keep on hand. It's great for moistening a lamb roast or making gravy for mashed potatoes. Of course, it's also delicious in soups and stews.*

¼ cup olive oil

3 pounds lamb bones

1¼ gallons water

2 carrots, roughly chopped

2 stalks celery, roughly chopped

1 onion, roughly chopped

⅓ cup white balsamic vinegar

1 cup chopped fresh flat leaf or curly parsley

1–2 bay leaves

1 teaspoon dried or 2 sprigs fresh thyme

2 teaspoons sea salt, or to taste

1 teaspoon freshly ground black pepper or 2 teaspoons peppercorns, or to taste

2 tomatoes, roughly chopped, or 2 tablespoons tomato paste

1  In a large stockpot over medium–low heat, gently heat the oil. Add the lamb bones and sauté for 5 to 7 minutes, until the bones have browned slightly. Remove from the heat.

2  Add the water and the vegetables to the pot and return it to medium–high heat. Bring to a boil.

3  Reduce the heat to medium–low and add the vinegar, herbs, salt, black pepper, and tomatoes or tomato paste (if using tomato paste, stir well to combine). Simmer, uncovered, for 4 hours, skimming off any film that rises to the surface at 15- to 20-minute intervals. Remove from the heat and set aside to cool to room temperature.

4  Using a fine sieve, strain out and discard any food solids, herbs, and spices.

5  Store in a tightly sealed, food-safe glass container. Store in the refrigerator for 1 week or in the freezer for a few months. Before using, be sure to skim any accumulated fat from the surface.

# CHAPTER 6

# Cheese, Cream, and Yogurt

M AKING YOUR OWN CHEESE AND DAIRY PRODUCTS may seem like something only artisans do, but you can easily do it, too, and you'll likely find it rewarding. Many markets today offer a wonderful variety of cheeses from around the world and I enjoy them immensely, but some of the more delicate and creamy cheeses are so easy to make at home that it's a shame not to learn how. When I make cheeses, I don't have to wonder whether the rennet and enzymes used are made with questionable animal by-products. Even if that isn't a concern for you, these cheeses taste incredible when you make them yourself, and they're much easier on the budget, too. Once you learn how to make them, it's a skill you'll treasure.

# Mascarpone Cheese

*This thick and silky Italian cream cheese isn't very sweet, so consider adding a little honey or sugar before using it in a recipe or just as a topping. It's often quite expensive to buy prepared, but it's surprisingly easy to make at home. It's commonly used to make tiramisù, but it's also wonderful on bread with jam or honey. Instead of discarding the leftover whey, use it to thicken soups or smoothies.*

**1 quart heavy whipping cream**

**2 tablespoons fresh lemon juice**

1 In a medium deep-bottomed saucepan or Dutch oven over low heat, warm the cream. Slowly raise the heat until the cream reaches 190°F.

2 Add the lemon juice and cook, whisking constantly, for 5 minutes, until the cream has thickened. Remove from the heat and set aside to cool to room temperature for 45 minutes.

3 Place an empty bowl in the sink. Drape a large piece of cheesecloth over it. Depress the cheesecloth a bit, so there's room to pour in the mixture and let it sit, and use a large rubber band or kitchen twine to secure the cheesecloth in place.

4 Slowly pour the cream mixture over the cheesecloth, taking care to ensure that it does not run over the rim of the bowl. Cover with a plate and refrigerate 8 to 12 hours or overnight to allow the whey to strain out of the mixture.

5 Lift the plate from the bowl and check the mascarpone cheese; you will know it is ready when its texture is silky and resembles that of soft cream cheese. Transfer the mascarpone cheese to an airtight container and store in the refrigerator. You can retain the whey (the liquid at the bottom of the bowl) for other uses. The cheese and whey will remain fresh in the refrigerator for about 1 week. Do not freeze.

# Ricotta Cheese

*You'll never have to worry about running to the store for ricotta cheese once you've mastered this recipe. It's super quick and much easier than you might think. You can find the citric acid, which is used to curdle the milk, in the spice aisle at most grocery stores.*

**½ gallon whole milk**

**½ cup heavy cream**

**1 teaspoon citric acid**

**½ teaspoon sea salt**

1 In a medium deep-bottomed saucepan or Dutch oven over medium–high heat, combine the milk and cream. Add the citric acid and salt and whisk vigorously until well combined. Continue stirring constantly as you cook. After 2 to 3 minutes, small curds will begin to form on the surface of the mixture. Soon thereafter, the mixture will take on a grayish color, and the curds will separate from the whey entirely. Remove from the heat.

2 Drape a large piece of cheesecloth over a colander. Depress the cheesecloth a bit, so there's room to pour in the mixture and let it sit, and use a large rubber band or kitchen twine to secure the cheesecloth in place. Place the colander over a bowl.

3 Slowly pour the milk mixture over the cheesecloth, taking care to ensure that it does not run over the rim of the bowl. Set aside to drain for 5 to 10 minutes.

4 Remove the whey from the bowl. Lift the edges of the cheesecloth and bring all 4 corners together. Twist the corners together tightly, forming a ball of cheese at the bottom (take care to push down any cheese that comes up to the neck of the cloth). Tie securely with a rubber band or kitchen twine. Return to the colander-lined bowl and refrigerate 8 hours or overnight to allow the whey to drain completely.

5 Open the cheesecloth. Transfer the ricotta cheese to an airtight container and store in the refrigerator. It will remain fresh in the refrigerator for about 1 week. Do not freeze.

YIELD: 3 CUPS

SPECIAL EQUIPMENT: Stand mixer fitted with the whisk attachment or a whisk

# Fresh Table Cream (Crème Fraîche)

*Fresh table cream, also referred to as crème fraîche, is a wonderfully versatile ingredient. It can be used to make your soups silky smooth and your cakes unbelievably moist. It's also wonderful paired with bread, honey, and jam, as it's similar to the delicious flavor of mascarpone but not as thick. It's also an ideal substitute for yogurt and cream cheese in some recipes.*

**2 cups buttermilk**

**1 cup heavy whipping cream**

1  In the chilled bowl of a stand mixer fitted with the whisk attachment or with a hand whisk, beat together the buttermilk and cream for 3 to 4 minutes, until the mixture begins to foam and thicken just slightly. Turn off the mixer.

2  Transfer the mixture to an airtight container and set aside at room temperature for 6 to 8 hours or overnight. The mixture will thicken to the consistency of thick yogurt or lightly whipped cream cheese. Transfer the mixture to a clean airtight container and store in the refrigerator. It will remain fresh in the refrigerator for 1½ to 2 weeks. Do not freeze.

YIELD: 12 CUPS

SPECIAL EQUIPMENT: Candy or digital-read thermometer, whisk

# Plain Whole Milk Yogurt

*You don't have to be a seasoned home cook or buy any fancy gadgets to make your own yogurt. Once you've done it the first time, save some to make another fresh batch. One word of caution: If this is your first time making yogurt, be sure to use extremely fresh storebought yogurt or buy a yogurt starter in order to be sure it has live cultures.*

½ gallon whole milk

½ cup storebought plain whole milk yogurt with live cultures

1   In a medium deep-bottomed saucepan or Dutch oven over medium heat, with a candy or digital-read thermometer inserted, bring the milk to temperature until bubbles begin to form. Slowly raise the heat until the milk reaches 175°F to 185°F. Reduce the heat to low and carefully monitor the milk's temperature as it falls. Once it reaches the range of 100°F to 115°F, vigorously whisk in the yogurt. Remove from the heat.

2   Transfer the mixture to an oven-safe container with a tight-fitting lid. Place the container in an oven preheated to 100°F or place it in the warmest spot in your kitchen. If leaving on a counter, wrap the container in a large cotton towel. Leave there, covered, for 6 to 10 hours or overnight (or slightly longer for thicker yogurt); do not remove the lid during this period of time.

3   Remove the container's lid and check to ensure that the proper consistency has been achieved. Transfer the mixture to an airtight container and store in the refrigerator. It will remain fresh in the refrigerator for 2 weeks. Do not freeze.

APRICOT YOGURT

BERRY "FROZEN" YOGURT

COCONUT YOGURT

YIELD: 1 SERVING

SPECIAL EQUIPMENT: 1 (16-ounce) glass Mason jar with lid (if using), whisk

# Apricot Yogurt

*Fruit-flavored yogurt varieties are abundant at the grocery store, but you can get an even fresher product by making it yourself at home. Start out with several batches early in the week and you'll have a different one each day as a perfect breakfast, lunch, or afternoon snack on the go.*

**¾ cup Plain Whole Milk Yogurt (see recipe on p. 39)**

**⅛ cup reduced-sugar apricot preserves**

1   In a small container with a tight-fitting lid or a Mason jar, place the yogurt. Using a fork or small whisk, blend in the apricot preserves. (You may also choose to add the apricot preserves to the container first and then add the yogurt, and stir together when ready to consume.)

2   Store in the refrigerator until ready to consume. Stays fresh for up to 1 week.

YIELD: 1¼ CUPS

SPECIAL EQUIPMENT: Food processor fitted with the "S" blade or blender

# Berry "Frozen" Yogurt

*This isn't exactly frozen yogurt, but the addition of frozen berries lends a slightly similar texture and makes a wonderful alternative to ice cream.*

**1 cup frozen strawberries and blueberries**

**1 cup Plain Whole Milk Yogurt (see recipe on p. 39)**

1   In the bowl of a food processor fitted with the "S" blade or a blender, combine the berries and the yogurt. Process or purée for 1 to 2 minutes, until thoroughly combined.

2   Serve immediately or transfer to an airtight container and freeze for up to 2 weeks.

# Coconut Yogurt

*It can be challenging to find coconut-flavored yogurt at the grocery store. You can make your own with little more than a good-quality coconut cream and/or a drop of Coconut Extract (recipe on p. 54).*

**1 cup Plain Whole Milk Yogurt (see recipe on p. 39)**

**¼ cup coconut cream**

**1 drop Coconut Extract (see recipe on p. 54) (optional)**

**2 tablespoons diced mango (optional)**

**2 tablespoons diced pineapple (optional)**

1   In a small mixing bowl, whisk together the yogurt, coconut cream, and Coconut Extract, if using.

2   Transfer to serving bowls or to an airtight container. Sprinkle on the diced fruit, if using. Store in the refrigerator; it will remain fresh in the refrigerator for 1 week. Do not freeze.

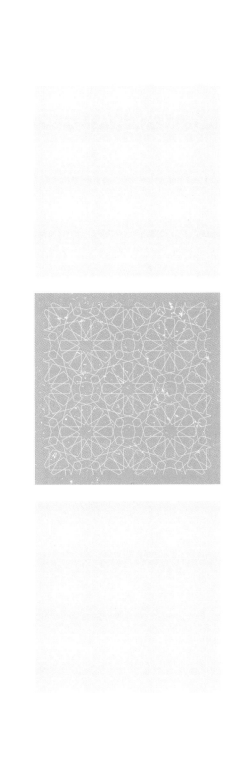

# CHAPTER 7

# Condiments and Salad Dressings

IF THERE ARE ANY HOMEMADE ITEMS I think every refrigerator should be stocked with, they're condiments and salad dressings. They're simple to make, and you can avoid all the unpronounceable preservatives and additives in many prepared varieties.

You'll find that if you set aside a short amount of time to make many of these useful condiments, you'll be so glad you did when it's time to use them.

**IN THIS CHAPTER**

YIELD: 1 CUP

SPECIAL EQUIPMENT: Heatproof glass or stainless steel mixing bowl, whisk

# Mayonnaise

*Storebought mayonnaise has lots of added emulsifiers to keep the consistency right. You'll find that your homemade mayonnaise will be much yellower than what you're used to, because eggs are the sole emulsifier.*

2 cups water + 3 tablespoons water, divided

2 whole large eggs

¼ cup white balsamic vinegar

1 teaspoon ground mustard

1 teaspoon light brown sugar or raw cane sugar

½ teaspoon fine sea salt

⅛ teaspoon freshly ground black pepper

2 tablespoons extra virgin olive oil

1   Place the 2 cups of water in a medium saucepan over medium–high heat and bring to a boil. Place a medium heatproof glass or stainless steel mixing bowl on top of the boiling water and combine the eggs, vinegar, and remaining 3 tablespoons of water in the bowl. Vigorously whisk the mixture until it thickens. Remove the bowl from the top of the saucepan and set aside.

2   In a small mixing bowl, stir together the mustard, sugar, salt, and black pepper. Transfer this mixture to the bowl containing the egg mixture and whisk together until thoroughly combined.

3   While continuously whisking, slowly drizzle the oil into the bowl.

4   Use immediately or transfer to an airtight container and refrigerate for up to 1 week.

YIELD: 1 CUP

SPECIAL EQUIPMENT: Food processor fitted with the "S" blade or blender, whisk

# "Dijon" Mustard

*Dijon is a quaint town in France's Burgundy region. I stumbled upon it during my college years and stuck around for a while to tour it. At the time, I had no idea that the town was famous for its mustard made with local wine. To get a similar taste without the addition of alcohol, I add a few key ingredients to dress up basic yellow mustard. You can easily double or triple this recipe, or add more mustard seeds if you prefer grainier mustard.*

½ cup yellow mustard

1 tablespoon honey

1 teaspoon + ⅓ cup white grape juice, divided (not from concentrate)

1 teaspoon red mustard seeds

1 teaspoon raw cane sugar

1 tablespoon minced green onion or yellow onion

1 teaspoon minced garlic

1 teaspoon light brown sugar

1  In a small mixing bowl, whisk together the mustard, honey, 1 teaspoon grape juice, mustard seeds, and cane sugar. Cover with plastic wrap and refrigerate for 2 days.

2  In a small saucepan over medium–high heat, combine the green onion, garlic, brown sugar, and remaining ⅓ cup grape juice. Bring to a boil and then immediately remove from the heat. Set aside to cool completely.

3  In the bowl of a food processor fitted with the "S" blade or a blender, combine the contents of the mixing bowl and the saucepan. Process or purée for 30 seconds, until thoroughly combined.

4  Use immediately or transfer to an airtight container and refrigerate for up to 2 weeks.

1 cup mayonnaise

¼ cup ketchup

2 tablespoons minced green bell pepper

2 tablespoons diced kosher pickle

1 hard-boiled egg, thinly chopped

1 tablespoon minced yellow onion

½ teaspoon freshly ground black pepper

¼ teaspoon thick hot sauce

¼ teaspoon fine sea salt

# Thousand-Island Dressing

*As a kid, I didn't really like Thousand-Island Dressing, but I grew to like it on sandwiches as an adult. Now that I know how to make it at home, I'd never consider storebought versions. Try it on burgers, fish sandwiches, and of course, your favorite salads.*

1  In a large mixing bowl, combine all the ingredients. Stir until well blended.

2  Use immediately or transfer to an airtight container and refrigerate for up to 1 week.

YIELD: 2½ CUPS

# Buttermilk Ranch Dressing

*This dressing is one of my favorites. I love it on salads and also on my Gyro Calzones (see recipe on p. 79). It easily doubles if you'll need more for a crowd.*

1½ cups Plain Whole Milk Yogurt (see recipe on p. 39)

½ cup buttermilk

½ cup heavy whipping cream

1 teaspoon freshly ground black pepper, or to taste

½ teaspoon fine sea salt, or to taste

1  In a large mixing bowl, combine all the ingredients. Stir until well blended.

2  Use immediately or transfer to an airtight container and refrigerate for up to 1 week.

YIELD: 1 CUP
SPECIAL EQUIPMENT: 1 (16-ounce) glass Mason jar with lid or shaker, whisk

# Sweet Italian Vinaigrette Dressing

*When I was a child, my mother and grandmother made salad dressing in a jar with oil, vinegar, and a storebought packet of dried herbs and seasonings. When I was on my own, I started to experiment with my own combinations of fresh and dried herbs. This is now the dressing my family loves best; we always have it on hand, especially in the summertime. Whenever I have lemons, I use their fresh squeezed juice in place of the vinegar. Use it on your favorite salad greens, caprese salad, or a sandwich.*

¼ cup balsamic vinegar

2 tablespoons honey

1 teaspoon dried or 2 teaspoons minced fresh curly parsley

1 teaspoon dried or 2 teaspoons minced fresh oregano

¼ teaspoon fine sea salt

¾ cup extra virgin olive oil

1  In a Mason jar or shaker, whisk together the vinegar, honey, parsley, oregano, and salt.

2  While whisking constantly, slowly drizzle the oil into the container. Continue whisking vigorously until the mixture is well combined and emulsified.

3  Use immediately or transfer to an airtight container and refrigerate for up to 1 week if using fresh herbs or 2 weeks if using dried herbs. Allow to rise to room temperature and shake vigorously before using.

YIELD: 1½ CUPS

SPECIAL EQUIPMENT: 1 (16-ounce) glass Mason jar with lid or shaker, whisk

# French Vinaigrette Dressing

*This is a lighter version of my Sweet Italian Vinaigrette Dressing (see recipe on p. 49). The addition of tarragon gives it a quintessentially French flavor.*

1 teaspoon superfine cane sugar

1 teaspoon ground mustard

¾ teaspoon fine sea salt

½ teaspoon minced yellow onion

½ teaspoon minced garlic

¼ teaspoon freshly ground black pepper

½ cup white balsamic or tarragon vinegar

2 teaspoons fresh lemon juice

1 cup light olive oil

1  In a Mason jar or shaker, combine the sugar, mustard, salt, onion, garlic, and black pepper.

2  Add the vinegar and lemon juice to the jar and whisk until well combined. While whisking constantly, slowly drizzle the oil into the container until the mixture is well combined and emulsified.

3  Use immediately or transfer to an airtight container and refrigerate for 2 to 3 weeks. Allow to rise to room temperature and shake vigorously before using.

# Creamy Honey Mustard Dressing

*This dressing isn't just for salads—it's also great to serve on cooked meats. You can easily double the recipe so you can keep plenty on hand.*

½ cup spicy mustard

¼ cup raw or regular honey

1 cup extra virgin olive oil

2 teaspoons fresh minced or ½ teaspoon freeze-dried shallots

1 teaspoon dried dill weed

1 teaspoon dried parsley

½ teaspoon fine sea salt

1  In a Mason jar or shaker, whisk together the mustard and honey.

2  While whisking constantly, slowly drizzle the oil into the container. Continue whisking vigorously until the mixture is well combined and emulsified.

3  Add the shallots, dill, parsley, and salt. Shake vigorously until well combined.

4  It is best to wait about 30 minutes to let the flavors combine before using. Transfer to an airtight container and refrigerate for up to 3 weeks. Allow to rise to room temperature and shake vigorously before using.

CHAPTER 8

# Flavor Extracts

FLAVOR EXTRACTS, WHEN NOT MADE SYNTHETICALLY, are often made by extracting flavor from a particular substance—say, an orange peel or a vanilla bean—by soaking it in alcohol. The alcohol leaches out, or extracts, the flavor and is then strained and bottled as a flavored extract. Although not enough to intoxicate a person when used in baking or cooking, one 4- to 8-ounce bottle could contain as much as 35% alcohol. You can instead use the following homemade extracts, which are of course alcohol free, for cooking, baking, and making beverages.

You'll be able to find places to purchase the vegetable glycerin and other items needed to make these extracts at home in the Resources section on page 200.

**IN THIS CHAPTER**

YIELD: 4 OUNCES

SPECIAL EQUIPMENT: 1 (16-ounce) glass Mason jar with lid, 1 (4-ounce) dark amber glass bottle with tight-fitting lid

# Almond Extract

**1 cup tap water**

**1 cup whole almonds**

**½ cup food-grade vegetable glycerin**

**¼ cup filtered water**

1  In a small saucepan over medium–high heat, bring the tap water to a rolling boil. Add the almonds and cook for 5 minutes. Remove from the heat, drain, and set aside to cool for 15 minutes, until they are easy to handle.

2  Remove and discard the skins from the almonds.

3  In a 16-ounce Mason jar, combine the almonds, glycerin, and filtered water. Tightly seal the lid of the jar and shake vigorously for 1 minute. Label the jar, taking care to include the date, and store in a cool, dry place for 1 month. Shake vigorously for 1 minute at least once a week during the storage period.

4  Place a small strainer over a large measuring cup and pour the contents of the Mason jar through the strainer. Transfer the liquid in the measuring cup to a 4-ounce dark amber glass bottle with a tight-fitting lid and discard the almonds.

5  Store the bottle in a cool, dry, and dark place and use as directed in recipes calling for almond extract.

YIELD: 4 OUNCES

SPECIAL EQUIPMENT: 1 (16-ounce) glass Mason jar with lid, 1 (4-ounce) dark amber glass bottle with tight-fitting lid

# Coconut Extract

**¾ cup food-grade vegetable glycerin**

**½ cup desiccated coconut chips or large flakes**

**¼ cup filtered water**

1  In a 16-ounce Mason jar, combine the glycerin, coconut chips, and filtered water. Tightly seal the lid of the jar and shake vigorously for 1 minute. Label the jar, taking care to include the date, and store in a cool, dry place for 1 month. Shake vigorously for 1 minute at least once a week during the storage period.

2  Place a small strainer over a large measuring cup and pour the contents of the Mason jar through the strainer. Transfer the liquid in the measuring cup to a 4-ounce dark amber glass bottle with a tight-fitting lid and discard the coconut.

3  Store the bottle in a cool, dry, and dark place and use as directed in recipes calling for coconut extract.

YIELD: 4 OUNCES

SPECIAL EQUIPMENT: 1 (8-ounce) glass Mason jar with lid, 1 (4-ounce) dark amber glass bottle with tight-fitting lid

# Lemon Extract

**⅓ cup food-grade vegetable glycerin**

**Peel of 4 lemons (about ⅓ cup), all white pith removed**

**3 tablespoons filtered water**

1 In an 8-ounce Mason jar, combine the glycerin, lemon peel, and filtered water. Tightly seal the lid of the jar and shake vigorously for 1 minute. Label the jar, taking care to include the date, and store in a cool, dry place for 1 month. Shake vigorously for 1 minute at least once a week during the storage period.

2 Place a small strainer over a large measuring cup and pour the contents of the Mason jar through the strainer. Transfer the liquid in the measuring cup to a 4-ounce dark amber glass bottle with a tight-fitting lid and discard the lemon peel.

3 Store the bottle in a cool, dry, and dark place and use as directed in recipes calling for lemon extract.

YIELD: 4 OUNCES

SPECIAL EQUIPMENT: 1 (16-ounce) glass Mason jar with lid, 1 (4-ounce) dark amber glass bottle with tight-fitting lid

# Mint Extract

**1 cup food-grade vegetable glycerin**

**1 cup fresh peppermint leaves**

**¼ cup filtered water**

1 In a 16-ounce Mason jar, combine the glycerin, peppermint leaves, and filtered water. Take care to press down on the mint leaves, making sure they are all under the glycerin. Tightly seal the lid of the jar and shake vigorously for 1 minute. Label the jar, taking care to include the date, and store in a cool, dry place for 1 month. Shake vigorously for 1 minute at least once a week during the storage period.

2 Place a small strainer over a large measuring cup and pour the contents of the Mason jar through the strainer. Transfer the liquid in the measuring cup to a 4-ounce dark amber glass bottle with a tight-fitting lid and discard the peppermint leaves.

3 Store the bottle in a cool, dry, and dark place and use as directed in recipes calling for mint extract.

YIELD: 4 OUNCES
SPECIAL EQUIPMENT: 1 (16-ounce) glass Mason jar with lid, 1 (4-ounce) dark amber glass bottle with tight-fitting lid

# Orange Extract

**½ cup food-grade vegetable glycerin**

**Peel of 4 oranges (about ½ cup), all white pith removed**

**¼ cup filtered water**

1   In a 16-ounce Mason jar, combine the glycerin, orange peel, and filtered water. Tightly seal the lid of the jar and shake vigorously for 1 minute. Label the jar, taking care to include the date, and store in a cool, dry place for 1 month. Shake vigorously for 1 minute at least once a week during the storage period.

2   Place a small strainer over a large measuring cup and pour the contents of the Mason jar through the strainer. Transfer the liquid in the measuring cup to a 4-ounce dark amber glass bottle with a tight-fitting lid and discard the orange peel.

3   Store the bottle in a cool, dry, and dark place and use as directed in recipes calling for orange extract.

YIELD: 4 OUNCES
SPECIAL EQUIPMENT: 1 (8-ounce) glass Mason jar with lid, 1 (4-ounce) dark amber glass bottle with tight-fitting lid

# Vanilla Extract

*This extract is probably the one you'll use most. Be sure to purchase high-quality vanilla beans, such as Bourbon beans. They are unrelated to the alcoholic beverage of the same name; instead, the name refers to all vanilla beans grown in Madagascar and other Indian Ocean islands. Suggested vendors are listed in the Resources section at the end of this book.*

**½ cup food-grade vegetable glycerin**

**2 Bourbon vanilla bean pods, slit lengthwise and sliced into 1-inch pieces**

**¼ cup filtered water**

1   In an 8-ounce Mason jar, combine the glycerin, vanilla bean pieces, and filtered water. Tightly seal the lid of the jar and shake vigorously for 1 minute. Label the jar, taking care to include the date, and store in a cool, dry place for 1 month. Shake vigorously for 1 minute at least once a week during the storage period.

2   Place a small strainer over a large measuring cup and pour the contents of the Mason jar through the strainer. Transfer the liquid in the measuring cup to a 4-ounce dark amber glass bottle with a tight-fitting lid and discard the vanilla beans.

3   Store the bottle in a cool, dry, and dark place and use as directed in recipes calling for vanilla extract.

# CHAPTER 9

# Bread, Pizza, and Pie Crust

THERE'S NOTHING QUITE LIKE HOMEMADE BREAD, pie crust, and pizza dough. I can easily tell the difference from storebought, as I've been fortunate to enjoy homemade for much of my life. My Sicilian grandmother made her own bread and pizza crust from scratch; to this day, the smell of yeast, fresh bread, or a pizza baking in the oven reminds me of her relentless efforts to feed her large family, her neighbors, and her friends the very best pizzas and bread this side of Sicily. For years, her recipes were a mystery to me; to be honest, they still are, because I never could quite document all the measurements during our phone conversations, but at least she talked me through her processes. That gave me enough information to experiment with the recipes and try them over and over again until I came up with recipes that achieve a taste close enough to what I remember, yet with added characteristics of the flavors I've encountered during my own travels in Italy.

Most storebought versions of breads, pizza doughs, and pie crusts have way too many ingredients, in my opinion. Real bread the world over is only made with a few all-natural ingredients, so why add ones with names we can hardly pronounce or that don't reveal their true origin?

One common ingredient in commercial breads, a dough conditioner called L-cysteine on most food labels, is sometimes sourced from human hair and thus is not halal. Some pie crusts contain lard, which is a natural ingredient—pork fat—but also not halal. Although it's possible today to find many all-natural, high-quality options, they can be difficult to find commercially and the artisan types, although wonderful, are often quite expensive for the average consumer.

The recipes in this chapter are meant to provide you with the basics you need to know for making your own bread, pizza dough, and pie crust. You'll be ready for family pizza night or to make a pie or loaf of bread to welcome new neighbors with something extra special and homemade.

Always be sure to buy the highest-quality ingredients you can find, as that is the best investment you can make in your recipes. See the Resources section on p. 200 for my recommendations.

**IN THIS CHAPTER**

YIELD: 1 LOAF

SPECIAL EQUIPMENT: Cooling rack, stand mixer fitted with the dough hook attachment

# Country Bread

*You can make homemade bread just like the ones you find at artisanal bakeries. It's not perfectly round, but it's crusty on the outside and light and fluffy on the inside. You'll love it with jams and the homemade cheese recipes in this book, but it's also hearty enough to make your favorite sandwiches, too.*

**2 cups all-purpose flour, divided**

**1 cup + ½ cup warm water, divided**

**1 tablespoon + 2 teaspoons active dry yeast**

**1 tablespoon raw cane sugar**

**2¾ cups whole-wheat flour**

**2½ tablespoons + ½ teaspoon sea salt**

**Cornmeal, for dusting**

1  In the bowl of a stand mixer with no attachment fitted, combine 1 cup of the all-purpose flour with 1 cup of the warm water, the yeast, and the sugar. Cover the bowl with a dry kitchen towel and set aside in the warmest spot in your kitchen for 15 minutes.

2  In a medium mixing bowl, combine the remaining 1 cup all-purpose flour with the whole-wheat flour and the salt.

3  Remove the towel from the bowl of the stand mixer, insert the dough hook attachment, and start running the stand mixer on low speed. Slowly add the contents of the medium mixing bowl and the remaining ½ cup of warm water to the bowl of the running stand mixer in thirds, alternating back and forth, making sure to end with the mixture in the mixing bowl. Mix for 3 to 4 minutes, until thoroughly combined and the dough is somewhat thickened. Turn off the mixer.

4  Turn out the dough onto a floured work surface. Using your hands, round out the dough into an oval-shaped ball. Place the ball of dough in a well-greased bowl and turn it so all sides of the dough are greased. Cover with a dry kitchen towel and set aside to rest and rise in a warm, draft-free place for 2 hours, until the dough has doubled in size.

5  Preheat the oven to 400°F. Dust a baking sheet with cornmeal to give the bread some grit as it bakes.

6   Remove the dough from the bowl, return it to the floured work surface, and gently punch it down. Round it out nicely by tucking in its edges.

7   Place the round of bread dough on the prepared baking sheet. Using kitchen shears or scissors, make an "X" mark in the middle of the top of the dough (it will allow some steam to escape as it bakes). Cover with the dry kitchen towel and set aside for 30 minutes.

8   Bake for 20 to 25 minutes, until the top and bottom of the loaf of bread are golden brown. Remove from the oven, remove from the baking sheet, and set aside on a wire rack to cool for 10 minutes.

9   Slice and serve.

YIELD: 2 CRUSTS
SPECIAL EQUIPMENT: *Pastry blender*

# Pie Crust

*I'd be the first to admit that it would be much easier to buy good-quality, all-natural, ready-made pie crusts. I've tried quite a few . . . but none can compare in taste or texture to the homemade ones you can make. Once you've prepared them, freeze them; you can defrost them and make a pie in no time. If a recipe calls for a double-crusted pie, this recipe is perfect—it yields 2 crusts, one for the bottom and one for the top of the pie.*

**2½ cups unbleached all-purpose flour**

**2 sticks unsalted butter, very cold and cut into small dice**

**1 teaspoon sea salt**

**1 teaspoon raw cane sugar**

**⅓ cup very cold water**

1   In a large mixing bowl, combine the flour, butter, salt, and sugar. Using your fingers, a pastry blender, or the tines of a fork, cut the butter into the flour mixture until a dough forms and most of the lumps are gone.

2   Add the water and knead the dough with your hands, shaping it into a ball. Cut it in half and re-form each half into a ball or a flat disc.

3   Wrap each dough ball or disc in plastic and refrigerate for at least 30 minutes before rolling it out. It should be very cold when it is rolled out and formed into a crust.

**COOKS' NOTES**

When you are ready to make a pie, follow the recipe directions. The crust should be very cold, but not frozen.

To blind bake the crust, place it in a pie pan. Using a fork, poke holes in it, or fill the crust with pie weights or unsoaked lentils or beans in order to prevent it from puffing as it bakes. Bake at 375°F for 20 minutes.

YIELD: 1 CRUST

SPECIAL EQUIPMENT: Stand mixer fitted with the dough hook attachment

# Pizza Crust

*Once you get this recipe down, pizza nights at home will be stress free. You know exactly what your family is eating and don't have to worry about cross-contamination of non-halal ingredients from outside pizza or how healthy the dough and other ingredients are.*

1 cup warm water

2 teaspoons active dry yeast

½ teaspoon raw cane sugar

2½ cups unbleached all-purpose flour, divided

¼ teaspoon sea salt

2 tablespoons extra virgin olive oil, plus more for greasing

Cornmeal, for dusting

1   In the bowl of a stand mixer with no attachment fitted, combine the warm water, yeast, and sugar. Mix with a fork until the yeast and sugar have dissolved. Cover the bowl with a dry kitchen towel and set aside in the warmest spot in your kitchen for 10 minutes.

2   Remove the towel from the bowl of the stand mixer, insert the dough hook attachment, and start running the stand mixer on low speed. Slowly add the ½ cup of the flour, the salt, and 2 tablespoons of the oil to the bowl of the running stand mixer. Mix for 3 to 4 minutes, until thoroughly combined.

3   As the mixer continues to run, add the remaining flour, ½ cup at a time, and mixing for about 1 minute after each addition.

4   Continue kneading the flour until all the flour has been integrated into the dough. (In the event that the dough fails to form into a perfect ball, you can remove the bowl from the stand mixer, add a little oil to your hands, and then work the dough inside the bowl, scraping up any flour on the sides and bottom of the bowl. Form the dough into a ball using your hands. Add more oil to your hands, if necessary, but only a little bit at a time. Keep mixing and kneading with your hands on a flat surface until the dough forms into a ball.) Place the ball of dough in a well-greased bowl and turn it so all sides of the dough are greased. Cover with a dry kitchen towel and set aside to rest and rise in a warm, draft-free place for 1 hour.

5 Turn out the dough onto a floured work surface. Using your hands, round out the dough into an oval-shaped ball. Place the ball of dough in a well-greased bowl and turn it so all sides of the dough are greased. Cover with a dry kitchen towel and set aside to rest and rise in a warm, draft-free place for 1 hour.

6 Using a floured rolling pin, roll out the dough into a 1-inch-thick, 14-inch diameter circle. See the pizza recipes on pp. 74-76 for directions on topping and preparation.

# CHAPTER 10

# American Cuisine

Certain American dishes I grew up with will always be comfort food to me. I have wonderful memories of summertime picnics in parks on or near Lake Erie that would not have been complete without burgers and hot dogs on the grill, macaroni and potato salads, huge slices of watermelon, and plenty of Frisbee, Wiffle ball, and swimming. Although my grandparents on both sides of my family had their own delicious ethnic dishes on hand at these picnics, everyone at our family gatherings enjoyed traditional all-American fare, too. It wouldn't have been a summertime or holiday celebration without it all.

The ultimate American experience is incorporating the foodways of your various cultural influences alongside those burgers, hot dogs, and potato salads. This section focuses on some of my favorite American recipes that traditionally include non-halal ingredients customized to be completely halal so they can still be enjoyed by and the recipes can be passed down to another generation of American kids who can have the best of both worlds on a plate.

**IN THIS CHAPTER**

YIELD: 6 SERVINGS

# Oven-Roasted Asparagus Wrapped in Turkey Strips

*This dish is commonly made with pork bacon, but you can easily make it halal with substitutes like turkey, beef, or chicken strips. This recipe makes enough asparagus to serve it in bundles on a platter as a side dish, but you can also individually wrap the asparagus stalks and serve them as elegant appetizers at a small dinner party. An alternative to roasting in the oven is to throw them on the grill once they are seasoned and wrapped.*

**2 pounds fresh asparagus, woody stems trimmed and discarded**

**⅓ cup olive oil**

**1 teaspoon sea salt, plus more to taste if desired**

**1 teaspoon freshly ground black pepper**

**1 pound smoked turkey breakfast strips, patted dry**

**Juice of ½ lemon, for sprinkling**

**2 tablespoons chopped fresh flat leaf parsley, for garnish**

1   Preheat the oven to 400°F.

2   In a large mixing bowl, combine the asparagus with the oil, salt, and black pepper.

3   Group the asparagus into sets of 5 and wrap each set with 3 to 5 strips of turkey breakfast strips. Place on a baking sheet. Sprinkle each set again with the salt, to taste.

4   Roast for 15 minutes, until crunchy. (If the asparagus stalks are on the thin side, check for doneness at 2-minute intervals after 10 minutes.) Remove from the oven.

5   Transfer the asparagus bunches to a serving platter. Sprinkle with the lemon juice. Garnish with the parsley and more salt, if desired. Serve hot.

# Eggs Benedict with Hollandaise Sauce

*This recipe is traditionally served with Canadian bacon, but I've found a halal substitute I think you'll enjoy. This recipe makes a great breakfast or brunch, especially when you have overnight guests. The whole house can wake up to a really nice meal.*

1 teaspoon unsalted butter

4 slices beef bologna

4 whole large eggs

Sea salt, to taste

2 English muffins

1 recipe Hollandaise Sauce (see recipe on p. 123)

2 tablespoons chopped fresh chives, for garnish

Dash cayenne pepper, for garnish

1   In a medium skillet over medium heat, melt the butter. Add the bologna to the skillet and sauté for 2 minutes, until browned. Repeat until both sides of each piece are browned. Remove from the heat and set aside.

2   In a deep-bottomed sauté pan over medium heat, bring 2 inches of water to a slow boil. Slowly add each egg, 1 at a time, to the boiling water. Reduce the heat to medium–low and lightly sprinkle the eggs with the salt. Cover and cook for 2 to 3 minutes, until a thin film has covered each egg.

3   Toast the English muffins. Place ½ of each English muffin on 4 serving plates. Place a slice of the bologna on top of each muffin half.

4   Using a spatula or slotted spoon, gently remove each egg from the water. Drain off any excess water, and transfer 1 egg on top of the bologna slices on each of the serving plates. Drizzle a ladleful of the Hollandaise Sauce on each serving and garnish with the chives and cayenne pepper. Serve.

# "Bacon," Lettuce, and Tomato Sandwich

*Some people might cringe at the thought of giving up bacon, but nowadays there are many wonderful alternatives made with beef, lamb, or turkey. This is a classic bacon, lettuce, and tomato sandwich with a halal twist.*

**6 ounces beef breakfast strips**

**4 slices whole-grain sandwich bread, toasted**

**¼ cup Mayonnaise (see recipe on p. 46)**

**1 large tomato, thinly sliced**

**4 large lettuce leaves, cut in half**

1   Warm a cast-iron skillet or sauté pan over high heat. Once the skillet is very hot, add the beef breakfast strips. (No oil is needed, as the strips will cook in their own fat.) Cook for 3 to 5 minutes on each side, until the edges begin to brown and the meat begins to bubble. Remove from the heat and remove the strips to a paper towel–lined plate to drain any excess fat.

2   Spread 1 tablespoon of the Mayonnaise on each slice of bread. Add a few slices of tomatoes and a piece of lettuce to ½ of the bread slices, and then top each of those with 3 to 4 beef breakfast strips. Close each sandwich by topping with the remaining slices of bread.

3   Slice on the diagonal, if desired, and serve.

# Pizza Sauce

*This sauce is for the two pizza recipes that follow, but of course you can use it on any homemade pizza you'd like to make. This recipe makes enough to cover 1 medium crust.*

**For the Sauté Pan**

**2 tablespoons extra virgin olive oil**

**1½ cups diced green bell peppers**

**½ cup diced yellow onion**

**2 cloves garlic, minced**

**1 teaspoon dried parsley**

**½ teaspoon sea salt**

**For the Saucepan:**

**2 (8-ounce) cans no-salt-added tomato sauce**

**1 tablespoon raw cane sugar**

**1 tablespoon roughly chopped fresh basil leaves**

1  In a medium sauté pan over medium heat, gently warm the oil. Add the peppers and sauté for 1 minute, until slightly softened. Add the onion and cook for 1 minute, stirring constantly in order to blend the peppers and onion together.

2  Reduce the heat to low and add the garlic, parsley, and salt to the pan. Cook for 10 minutes. Remove from the heat and set aside.

3  In a medium saucepan over low heat, combine the tomato sauce, sugar, and basil. Transfer the contents of the sauté pan into the saucepan, stir, and cook, covered, for 40 minutes. Remove from the heat and set aside to cool to room temperature before using.

YIELD: 6 SERVINGS

SPECIAL EQUIPMENT: Pizza pan or baking sheet, stand mixer fitted with the dough hook attachment

# Beef Pepperoni Pizza

*It was many years after I began eating halal that I found a good-quality beef pepperoni substitute for my pizza recipes. Now there are many to choose from. I prefer to stay away from any that have nitrites or nitrates, but that can be quite a challenge at times. You should be able to find sejouk, the Turkish-style hot sausage, or something similar, in most Middle Eastern and Mediterranean markets.*

**Olive oil, for greasing**

**1 Pizza Crust (see recipe on p. 64)**

**1⅓ cups Pizza Sauce (see recipe on p. 74)**

**4 ounces fresh or shredded mozzarella cheese**

**¼ pound sejouk (spicy Turkish-style beef or beef and lamb) sausage, cut into 24 round pieces**

1  Preheat the oven to 450°F and grease a pizza pan or baking sheet with the oil. Set aside.

2  Transfer the Pizza Crust dough to the prepared pizza pan. Crimp the edges of the crust all the way around. Spread the Pizza Sauce evenly across the crust, leaving about 1 inch on the outside rim uncovered. Sprinkle the cheese and then the rounds of sejouk on top of the Pizza Sauce.

3  Bake for 15 minutes, until the cheese is slightly browned around the edges. Remove from the oven and set aside to cool for 10 minutes.

4  Slice and serve.

**RESOURCES**

I prefer Nema Stick Beef Soudjouk, (Hot) from Nema Food Company (nemahalal.com).

YIELD: 6 SERVINGS

SPECIAL EQUIPMENT: Pizza pan or baking sheet, stand mixer fitted with the dough hook attachment

# Hawaiian Pizza

*During my teenage years, my first real job at a local pizza restaurant exposed me to Hawaiian-style pizza, which was very popular with our customers. The version the restaurant made contained ham and bacon, so naturally I needed to come up with a halal substitute to replace those meats. I've found ground turkey is a nice complement to the pineapple, but ground beef may be just as good.*

**1 tablespoon olive oil, plus more for greasing**

**½ pound ground turkey**

**1 teaspoon sea salt**

**¼ teaspoon freshly ground black pepper**

**1 Pizza Crust (see recipe on p. 64)**

**1⅓ cups Pizza Sauce (see recipe on p. 74)**

**4 ounces shredded mozzarella cheese, plus more if desired**

**1 cup diced pineapple, drained**

**¼ cup roughly chopped fresh basil leaves**

1  Preheat the oven to 450°F and grease a pizza pan or baking sheet with the oil. Set aside.

2  In a medium sauté pan over medium heat, warm the remaining 1 tablespoon of oil. Add the turkey, season with the salt and black pepper, and cook, stirring occasionally, for 10 to 15 minutes, until well browned. Set aside to cool to room temperature.

3  Transfer the Pizza Crust dough to the prepared pizza pan. Crimp the edges of the crust all the way around. Spread the Pizza Sauce evenly across the crust, leaving about 1 inch on the outside rim uncovered. Sprinkle the cheese, pineapple, cooked turkey, and basil on top of the Pizza Sauce. (You can add a bit more cheese on top of these toppings if you like.)

4  Bake for 15 minutes, until the cheese is slightly browned around the edges (add 3 to 5 minutes to the baking time if you opt to add cheese over the toppings). Remove from the oven and set aside to cool for 10 minutes.

5  Slice and serve.

# Chicago-Style Pulled Beef Sandwiches

*Being a Chicago transplant means that I had to try the classic pulled beef sandwiches when I moved here, but eating out is nearly impossible as there are currently no halal restaurants that offer it. I think there should be! I know plenty of people who love serving these sandwiches at parties, so I decided to make a batch I knew I could serve to a small crowd. Don't skimp on the Beef Broth—it is very important for the dish's flavor.*

¼ cup olive oil

15 ounces hot or mild giardiniera (pickled vegetable relish), with juices and oils

3 tablespoons minced garlic

1 teaspoon freshly ground black pepper

¼ teaspoon sea salt

2 cups thinly sliced yellow onion

2 pounds boneless beef round, cubed and patted dry

1 recipe Beef Broth (see recipe on p. 31)

3 cups water, divided

4 hoagie rolls, sliced open and toasted

1   In a large, deep skillet or Dutch oven over medium heat, warm the oil. Add the giardiniera, garlic, black pepper, and salt and sauté for 5 minutes. Add the onions and sauté for 3 minutes, until they are nicely browned and translucent.

2   Add the beef round meat to the skillet and cook on 1 side for 5 minutes, until browned. Turn the cubes and repeat until all sides are browned.

3   Add the Beef Broth to the skillet, reduce the heat to low, and cook, covered, for 3 hours. After the first hour, add 2 cups of the water, and after the second hour, add the remaining 1 cup of water.

4   Remove from the heat. Using a large fork, pull the meat apart into small pieces.

5   Place a generous portion of the beef, vegetables, and juices on each of the toasted hoagie rolls and serve.

**RESOURCES**

I like La Campagna Hot Giardiniera and Marconi Hot Giardiniera.

YIELD: 4 SERVINGS
SPECIAL EQUIPMENT: 18-inch × 26-inch baking sheet

# Gyro Calzone

*This recipe is one of my all-time favorites. The pizza place I worked at as a teen used to make these, but I never knew how they made their dough—I only saw them put the calzones together and then sometimes got to taste the result, which was a real treat. Once I began cooking from scratch and had a great pizza crust recipe to work with, I decided to fulfill my craving for this special dish. You can double the pizza crust recipe as well as the ingredients listed below and make an even larger calzone for a crowd.*

1 recipe Pizza Crust (see recipe on p. 64)

Olive oil, for greasing

12 slices frozen lamb gyro meat

2 tablespoons cornmeal (optional)

2 tablespoons Mayonnaise (see recipe on p. 46)

½ cup thinly sliced cucumber

¼ cup thinly sliced yellow or white onion

4 leaves romaine or iceberg lettuce, thinly chopped

1 cup Buttermilk Ranch Dressing (see recipe on p. 48), for dipping

1   Roll the Pizza Crust dough out so it is large enough to fill an 18-inch × 26-inch rectangular baking sheet. Preheat the oven to 450°F and grease the baking sheet with the oil.

2   Place the dough over the baking sheet, arranging it so it covers the bottom of the sheet. Cover half of the dough with the slices of gyro meat, overlapping them a bit to create some bulk. Fold half of the dough over the top of the other half, covering it but leaving a little overlap so that the 2 edges don't stick together. Cut a small hole or "X" in the top of the dough to release steam as it cooks. Dust with the cornmeal, if using.

3   Bake on the top rack of the oven for 12 to 15 minutes or on the bottom rack for 20 minutes. Remove from oven and place on a cooling rack for 5 to 7 minutes.

4   Open the calzone and spread the Mayonnaise inside the top of it. Stuff the interior of the calzone with the cucumber, onion, and lettuce.

5   Close the calzone and slice into 8 pieces (3 lengthwise slices and 1 horizontal slice). Serve with the Buttermilk Ranch Dressing.

YIELD: 4 SERVINGS
SPECIAL EQUIPMENT: Whisk

# Clam Chowder

*I love a good clam chowder, but those served in restaurants are often made with bacon or served with bacon on top. My recipe features simple and light ingredients, the best clams around, and a halal substitute for bacon.*

**3–4 tablespoons unsalted butter, divided**

**½ cup diced beef or turkey breakfast strips**

**1⅓ cups peeled and diced Yukon gold potatoes**

**1 teaspoon sea salt**

**1 teaspoon freshly ground black pepper**

**½ cup diced celery**

**½ cup diced onion**

**1 cup roughly chopped shelled cherrystone clams**

**2 cups whole milk**

**1 cup water**

**½ cup heavy cream**

**1 tablespoon cornstarch dissolved in 1 tablespoon warm water**

**Oyster crackers, for topping**

**2 tablespoons chopped fresh flat leaf or 2 teaspoons dried parsley, for garnish**

1   In a large saucepan or medium Dutch oven over medium heat, warm 1 tablespoon of the butter if using beef strips or 2 tablespoons of the butter if using turkey strips. Add the beef strips to the pan and cook for 3 to 5 minutes on each side. Transfer the beef strips to a paper towel–lined plate to drain any excess fat.

2   Add 2 more tablespoons of the butter to the saucepan. Once the butter begins to froth, add the potatoes, salt, and black pepper. Sauté for 2 to 3 minutes, stirring constantly to prevent sticking, until the potatoes have browned on all sides. Add the celery and onion and sauté for 1 to 3 minutes, until they have softened.

3   Add the chopped clams to the saucepan and cook for 3 minutes. Add the milk, water, and cream and stir until combined, and cook for 5 to 7 minutes. Add the cornstarch–water slurry to the saucepan and whisk vigorously until the slurry is completely dissolved.

4   Return the beef strips to the saucepan and stir until thoroughly combined. Reduce the heat to low and simmer, uncovered, for 10 minutes. Remove from the heat.

5   Ladle the chowder into individual cups or bowls. Top with the oyster crackers and garnish with the parsley.

**RESOURCES**

You can purchase Maine Whole Cherrystone Clams at Trader Joe's.

# Beef Pot Roast

*Pot roast recipes might feature either beef or pork, but they almost always include wine. My version includes beef, of course, and a great halal substitute for the alcohol—grape juice! It's so versatile that if you serve it for dinner, you can slice up the leftovers for sandwiches the next day.*

¼ cup olive oil

3 pounds boneless beef chuck roast, patted dry

2 teaspoons sea salt

1 teaspoon freshly ground black pepper

3 cups quartered yellow onion

1 cup Beef Broth (see recipe on p. 31)

1 cup Concord grape juice (not from concentrate)

3 sprigs fresh thyme

2 bay leaves

8 cloves garlic, quartered

2 tablespoons tomato paste

10 small Yukon gold potatoes, quartered

6 carrots, each sliced on the diagonal into 4 pieces

1   Preheat the oven to 350°F.

2   In a Dutch oven over medium–high heat, warm the oil. Place the whole piece of beef in the Dutch oven and season with the salt and black pepper. Cook on 1 side for 5 minutes, until browned. Turn and repeat until all sides are browned.

3   Add the onions and sauté, stirring constantly to prevent sticking, for 5 to 7 minutes, until they have softened and are translucent. Add the Beef Broth, grape juice, thyme sprigs, and bay leaves. Stir in the garlic and tomato paste. Remove from the heat.

4   Cover the Dutch oven and place in the oven. Roast for 1½ hours.

5   Add the potatoes and carrots and return to the oven for 40 minutes. Remove and discard the bay leaves. Remove from the oven and set aside, covered, to let the meat rest for 10 minutes.

6   Slice the pot roast. Transfer the meat to a serving platter and surround it with the vegetables. Pour some of the juices from the Dutch oven over the meat and vegetables and transfer the rest to serve in a pitcher. Serve.

# Classic Meatloaf

*A quintessentially American dish, this meatloaf is super moist. Your family will love it served with mashed potatoes and creamed corn—a meal that always conjures up memories of the crisp air of fall for me. The secret to its moistness is the somewhat-Italian twist I give it by using ingredients from my homemade meatball recipes.*

Olive oil, for greasing

2 pounds ground beef

1 cup very fine breadcrumbs

⅔ cup freshly grated Parmesan cheese

4 whole large eggs

¼ cup chopped fresh parsley

4 cloves garlic, crushed

½ teaspoon sea salt

¼ teaspoon freshly ground black pepper

⅔ cup ketchup

3 tablespoons tomato paste

1   Preheat the oven to 350°F and grease a 10-inch × 6-inch loaf pan with the oil.

2   In a large mixing bowl, combine the ground beef, breadcrumbs, Parmesan cheese, eggs, parsley, garlic, salt, and black pepper. Using your clean hands or a stand mixer fitted with the paddle attachment, stir together until the meat mixture is very smooth and all the ingredients are well combined.

3   Transfer the meat mixture into the prepared loaf pan. Using a spatula, smooth the top of the meatloaf.

4   In a small mixing bowl, combine the ketchup and tomato paste. Using a spatula, evenly spread the ketchup mixture directly on top of the loaf. Tent with foil.

5   Bake, covered, for 1 hour and 10 minutes. Remove the foil tent and bake for 35 minutes. Using a meat thermometer inserted in the center of the loaf, ensure that the internal temperature of the loaf has reached 165°F. (If you do not have a meat thermometer, you can slice a small portion of the meatloaf and check to ensure that the juices run clear.) Remove from the oven and set aside to cool for 5 to 10 minutes.

6   Remove the meatloaf from the pan and transfer to a serving platter. Slice into generously sized pieces and serve.

**For the Chicken**

3 teaspoons olive oil

1 teaspoon unsalted butter

1 (about ¾ pound) large boneless skinless chicken breast

Sea salt, to taste

Freshly ground black pepper, to taste

**For the Salad**

6 slices beef breakfast strips

3 hard-boiled eggs, peeled

2 cups roughly chopped romaine lettuce

1½ cups diced roma tomatoes

2 cups roughly chopped endive

2 cups roughly chopped Boston lettuce

1 firm avocado, diced

½ cup crumbled blue cheese

**For the Dressing**

¼ cup balsamic vinegar

1 tablespoon mild (light) honey

1 clove garlic, minced

½ teaspoon dry mustard powder

Sea salt, to taste

Freshly ground black pepper, to taste

½ cup extra virgin olive oil

YIELD: 4 SERVINGS

SPECIAL EQUIPMENT: Whisk

# Cobb Salad with Beef Strips

*Most people who have grown up eating only halal meat may not have had the chance to try a really great Cobb salad, since they almost always feature bacon. With the right substitutes, anyone can enjoy this classic American salad that's truly a meal by itself.*

TO MAKE THE CHICKEN

1   In a small sauté pan with a lid over low heat, combine and gently warm the oil and butter.

2   Generously season the chicken with the salt and black pepper and place it into the sauté pan. Cook on 1 side for 3 to 5 minutes, until browned. Turn and repeat until all sides are browned.

3   Cover the pan and cook for 5 minutes, until the inside of the meat is thoroughly cooked. Remove from the heat.

4   Transfer the chicken to a cutting board and set aside to cool.

TO MAKE THE BEEF STRIPS AND ASSEMBLE THE SALAD

1   Place the beef strips in the sauté pan and return it to high heat. Cook for 3 to 5 minutes on each side, until the edges begin to brown and the meat begins to bubble. Remove from the heat and transfer the strips to a paper towel–lined plate to drain any excess fat.

2   Prepare a wide platter large enough to individually display all of the chopped ingredients (a long, wide, and rectangular platter works best).

3 Gently slice each of the eggs in ½. Using a small spoon, scoop out each of the cooked yolks without crumbling them, if possible. Cut each ½ of each yolk into 2 pieces and place them in a small bowl. Dice the egg whites and place them in a small bowl.

4 Dice the chicken breast and beef strips into small bite-size pieces and place them in 2 separate small bowls.

5 Line the left side of the platter with a row of the romaine lettuce in a vertical direction. Alongside it, add a row of the diced tomatoes. Next, add a row of the endive. Next to that row, add a row of the egg whites. Next, add a row of the Boston lettuce, and then 1 of the yolks. Last, add a row of the avocado.

6 Sprinkle the blue cheese, diced chicken, and diced beef strips on top of the rows of lettuce and endive.

TO MAKE THE DRESSING

1 In a small mixing bowl, combine the vinegar, honey, garlic, mustard powder, salt, and black pepper. Whisk until well combined. While continuing to whisk vigorously, drizzle the oil into the mixture. Continue whisking until the dressing is emulsified and thoroughly mixed.

TO SERVE THE SALAD

1 Either combine some of each ingredient on individual plates and serve with a side of dressing or pour the dressing over the entire salad and serve on the platter.

YIELD: 4 SERVINGS

SPECIAL EQUIPMENT: Mortar and pestle or food processor fitted with the "S" blade, pastry brush, whisk

# Oven-Roasted BBQ Beef Ribs

*If you've got a good halal butcher nearby, be sure to ask if he's got a rack of beef ribs in his inventory. If not, ask him to order them for you, as most butchers don't ordinarily stock them. I often show my butcher the recipe I'm making so he can better understand my needs—as with most things, communication is the key to good results.*

**15 cloves garlic**

**4 teaspoons sea salt**

**4 teaspoons freshly ground black pepper**

**3 teaspoons smoked paprika**

**2 teaspoons chili powder**

**1½ cups honey**

**3 tablespoons apple cider vinegar**

**4–6 pounds beef back ribs, patted dry**

1   Using a mortar and pestle or food processor fitted with the "S" blade, grind together the garlic, salt, black pepper, paprika, and chili powder. Continue grinding until the garlic has been completely integrated into the spices.

2   In a small mixing bowl, combine the garlic–spice mixture and the honey and stir until well blended. Whisk in the apple cider vinegar until thoroughly combined.

3   Using a pastry brush, coat both sides of the beef back ribs with ½ of the seasoning glaze. Cover with foil and refrigerate for 8 hours or overnight. Refrigerate the remaining seasoning glaze.

4   Preheat the oven to 300°F. Grease a roasting pan.

5   Coat the cold ribs with the remaining seasoning glaze. Place them in the prepared roasting pan, tent with foil, and roast for 2½ hours. Remove from the oven.

6   Remove the ribs from the roasting pan and set aside to rest on a platter or cutting board for 10 minutes.

7   Break up the ribs into individual servings. (It gets messy, so it's a good idea to have some wet cloths or wipes around!) Serve hot.

# Iced Coffee

*Cold coffee drinks are very popular, of course, but it can get pretty expensive to pick one up at a coffee shop every day on your way to work. You can easily make them at home without taking too much time. To add flavor, use the syrups I recommend in the Resources section.*

2 cups cold coffee

2 tablespoons + 1 teaspoon sweetened condensed milk

10 ice cubes

1  In a tall glass or large measuring cup, combine the coffee and condensed milk. Whisk until thoroughly combined.

2  Place the ice cubes in a tall cup with a lid. Close the lid and shake very well. Enjoy!

**COOKS' NOTES**

Don't forget a straw—it's more enjoyable and easier to drink it that way!

For a creamier taste, add 1 to 2 cups of chocolate ice cream.

YIELD: 4 ½ CUPS
SPECIAL EQUIPMENT: Blender

# Candy Bar Shake

*For a family who craves something a little different at dessert time, this shake, resembling some favorite American candy bars, just might do the trick.*

**2 apples, peeled and chopped**

**½ cup creamy unsalted peanut butter**

**¼ cup caramel flavored sauce, plus more for drizzling**

**2 cups vanilla ice cream**

**3 ice cubes**

**1 cup whole milk**

1 In the bottom of a blender, combine the apples, the peanut butter, and ¼ cup of the caramel. Place the ice cream and ice cubes on top and then pour the milk over the mixture. Blend on high for 45 seconds to 1 minute.

2 Pour into serving glasses and drizzle the remaining caramel on the top of each shake. Serve immediately or refrigerate; the consistency should remain the same until the next day.

**RESOURCES**

I like Monin Caramel Flavored Sauce, Trader Joe's Fleur de Sel Caramel Sauce, and Trader Joe's Creamy Unsalted Peanut Butter.

YIELD: 12 SERVINGS

SPECIAL EQUIPMENT: Food processor fitted with the "S" blade or blender, whisk

# Golden Peach Punch

*If you're ever in need of a great party drink for summer guests, this is it. It's refreshing, sweet, and captures the essence of seasonal summer fruits. It's a great choice for an eid party, as it can be placed in a large punch bowl and guests can serve themselves. It's best to prepare this just before guests arrive, as the sparkling water will lose its fizz if prepared in advance.*

4 very ripe peaches, peeled and pitted

1 quart white grape juice (not from concentrate)

2½ cups sparkling water

2 cups ice

6 strawberries, hulled and thinly sliced, for serving

1 peach, peeled, pitted, and sliced into rounds, for serving

1   Place the peaches in the bowl of a food processor fitted with the "S" blade or a blender. Purée them for 1 minute, until the texture is completely smooth.

2   In a large punch bowl, combine the grape juice and sparkling water. Add the peach purée and whisk until thoroughly combined.

3   Add the ice and float the strawberry slices and peach rounds on top of the punch. Serve.

# Spiced Mulled Cider

*This is the perfect party drink for entertaining in the fall. Many traditional recipes call for wine, but I've found a halal combination that provides both the fruity taste and deep color you'll want in your cider. Serve hot when friends and family come to visit and it's brisk but warm enough to sit outdoors by a fire.*

1½ quarts apple cider

1 quart Concord grape juice (not from concentrate)

1 cup honey

2 cinnamon sticks

1 navel orange and 1 tangerine, sliced about ½-inch thick

1 pear and 1 red apple, cored and sliced about ½-inch thick

1   In a medium stockpot over medium–high heat, combine the apple cider, grape juice, honey, cinnamon sticks, and sliced fruit. Bring to a boil, reduce the heat to medium–low, and simmer for 20 minutes.

2   Ladle ½ cup servings into small mugs and serve hot.

# Orange Fizz Cream Punch

*This great party punch reminds me of Dreamsicles, which I enjoyed as a kid. The wonderful mixture of orange and cream is so delicious. As with other drinks with sparkling water, this recipe should be prepared just before serving.*

1 quart sparkling water

Juice of 6 oranges

¼ cup + 2 tablespoons candied orange or mango syrup

1 quart French vanilla ice cream

1–2 cups ice

Freshly grated zest of 1 lime

1  In a large punch bowl, combine the sparkling water, orange juice, and syrup. Stir to combine.

2  Add the ice cream in scoops, taking care not to stir.

3  Gently add the ice and lime zest. Serve.

**RESOURCES**

Monin makes candied orange and mango syrups.

# Cherry Cheesecake Bites

*This is a great way to serve cheesecake at a party—in bite-size pieces, allowing you to easily feed a crowd. Served with fresh cherry syrup on top, it has all the taste of classic cherry cheesecake in small, guilt-free portions. Be sure to make the syrup first, as it needs to be chilled overnight.*

**For the Cherry Syrup**

**2 cups raw cane sugar**

**Juice of 1 lemon**

**2 tablespoons freshly grated lemon zest**

**1 teaspoon sea salt**

**½ cup cherry juice**

**½ cup water**

**2 pounds cherries, pitted**

**For the Crust**

**3 cups finely ground graham crackers**

**2 tablespoons raw cane sugar**

**1½ sticks unsalted butter, melted**

TO MAKE THE CHERRY SYRUP

1   In a medium saucepan over medium heat, combine the sugar, lemon juice and zest, and salt. Cook, stirring constantly, for 5 to 7 minutes.

2   Add the cherry juice and then the water to the saucepan, 1 at a time. Gently add the pitted cherries and stir, taking great care not to break the cherries. Bring to a boil and cook, stirring constantly, for 10 minutes.

3   Reduce the heat to medium–low and simmer for 30 minutes. Remove from the heat and set aside to cool to room temperature.

4   Refrigerate overnight before using.

TO MAKE THE CRUST

1   In a large mixing bowl, combine the graham crackers and sugar. Stir well and transfer to a 15-inch × 10-inch rectangular baking dish.

2   Add the melted butter to the dish and, using your fingers, integrate it into the graham cracker–sugar mixture. Press mixture into baking dish to form a crust that covers the entire bottom of the dish and goes up the sides slightly. Set aside.

## For the Filling

3 (8-ounce) packages cream cheese, at room temperature

1 cup raw cane sugar

3 egg yolks

¼ cup Fresh Table Cream (see recipe on p. 38)

5 whole large eggs

2 tablespoons freshly grated lemon zest

1 teaspoon Lemon Extract (see recipe on p. 55)

### TO MAKE THE FILLING

1  In the bowl of a stand mixer fitted with the paddle attachment, cream together the cream cheese and sugar on medium speed for 2 to 3 minutes. Scrape down the sides and bottom of the stand mixer bowl to prevent lumps from forming. Add the egg yolks and Fresh Table Cream and continue mixing on medium speed for 2 to 3 minutes, until well combined.

2  Reduce the mixer speed to low and add the eggs, 1 at a time and scraping down the sides of the bowl as you add them, to the stand mixer bowl. After each egg is added, mix on low speed for 1 to 2 minutes, until the mixture is well combined. As the stand mixer continues to run on low speed, add the lemon zest and extract to the bowl of the mixer.

3  Turn off the mixer and change to the whisk attachment. Beat on high speed for 10 minutes, until the mixture is completely smooth. Turn off the mixer.

### TO ASSEMBLE THE CHERRY CHEESECAKE BITES

1  Preheat the oven to 325°F.

2  Transfer the contents of the stand mixer bowl to the baking dish containing the crust. Place the baking dish on a baking sheet.

3  Place the baking sheet and dish on the top rack of the oven. On a lower rack, place an oven-safe dish filled with water (this will help prevent cracking on the top of the cheesecake). Bake for 45 to 50 minutes. Remove from the oven and set aside to cool to room temperature.

4  Refrigerate, uncovered, for at least 4 hours or until ready to serve.

5  If any condensation appears on the cheesecake, dry it with a paper towel before slicing. Slice the cake into 12 to 16 bite-size pieces and drizzle the Cherry Syrup on top of each piece.

6  Transfer each slice to a serving plate or a small cupcake liner.

# Mixed Berry Pie

*There's nothing quite like summer berries baked in a pie to celebrate the season. Of course, you can always freeze those summer berries so you can make this pie any time of year. This pie is especially delicious with a scoop of French vanilla ice cream.*

¼ cup raw cane sugar

¼ cup all-purpose unbleached flour

1 teaspoon ground cinnamon

Pinch sea salt

1 quart frozen mixed berries

1 teaspoon Lemon Extract (see recipe on p. 55) or freshly grated lemon zest

1 recipe Pie Crust (see recipe on p. 63)

1 whole large egg

1 tablespoon whole milk or water

1 Preheat the oven to 400°F.

2 In a small mixing bowl, combine the sugar, flour, cinnamon, and salt and mix with a fork until thoroughly combined.

3 In a large mixing bowl, combine the berries with the Lemon Extract or zest. Slowly add the contents of the small mixing bowl to the large mixing bowl in thirds, folding gently as you add and taking great care to leave the berries intact. Set aside.

4 Turn out the first Pie Crust dough ball or disc onto a floured work surface. Using a floured rolling pin, roll out the dough into a ⅛-inch-thick, 9-inch-diameter circle. This will serve as the top crust. Set aside.

5 Repeat with the second disc, rolling it out thinner and 4 inches larger in diameter so it will completely cover the bottom and sides of the pie pan and allow some dough to overlap with the top crust. Place this crust inside the pie pan.

6 Transfer the contents of the large mixing bowl to the pie pan, evenly spreading it in the dish. Place the top crust over the filling and crimp the edges together.

7    In a small mixing bowl, combine the egg and milk or water and mix well with a fork. Using a pastry brush, spread the egg wash over the top of the pie. Using a sharp, nonserrated knife, slice an "X" in the center of the pie to allow steam to release while baking.

8    Transfer the pie pan to a baking sheet and tent the pan with foil to prevent burning. Place the baking sheet and pie pan on the top rack of the oven and bake for 10 minutes.

9    Reduce the temperature to 350°F and bake for 45 minutes to 1 hour. Remove from the oven and set aside to cool to room temperature.

10   Slice and serve.

YIELD: 6–12 SERVINGS

# Creamy Marshmallow Treats

*Marshmallow treats are a favorite snack for kids and adults like me who grew up eating them, but I prefer this much creamier version to the dry, crunchy treats of my youth. The challenge is in finding good halal marshmallows. See p. 202 to discover two varieties I really like.*

**1 stick unsalted butter**

**20 ounces halal or vegan marshmallows**

**4 cups crisp rice cereal**

1 In a deep-bottomed saucepan or Dutch oven over medium heat, warm the butter. Once the butter is about halfway melted, add the marshmallows and cook, stirring constantly, for 5 minutes, until the marshmallows are completely melted. Remove from the heat and immediately add the cereal to the saucepan, stirring vigorously until well combined.

2 Transfer the contents of the saucepan to a 13-inch × 9-inch rectangular baking dish and smooth and level the mixture with a flat spatula. Cover with plastic wrap and refrigerate for 30 minutes, until set.

3 Slice into squares and serve.

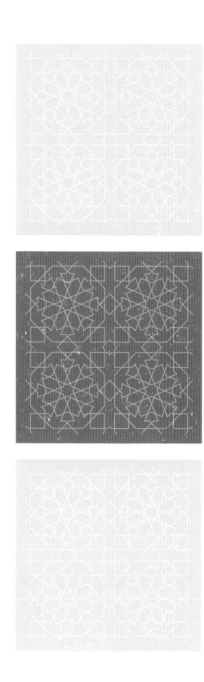

# CHAPTER 11

# Asian Cuisine

W HILE LIVING AND WORKING IN THE San Francisco Bay Area just after college, I quickly became exposed to the huge variety of authentic Asian cuisine available on the West Coast. I had dim sum in Chinatown, tea at the Japanese Gardens, shabu-shabu in LA's Little Tokyo, sushi as often as and whenever I could, and Korean and Thai food on a regular basis. I learned to love and appreciate all the complex flavors and spices that went into these dishes—certainly a very different experience than any of the Asian food I'd had during my childhood in the Midwest.

After becoming a Muslim and embracing a halal lifestyle, I quickly learned that eating Chinese, Japanese, Korean, or Thai food in restaurants would be challenging due to the heavy use of pork, non-*dhabiha* meats, and alcohol in dishes. On the flip side, I've been fortunate to have exceptional halal Chinese and Malay food at Mas' Chinese Islamic Restaurant in Anaheim, California, and at Usmania in Chicago's Devon Avenue neighborhood, but better yet, I've learned how to make many of my family's favorite restaurant-style Asian dishes myself. I've developed the following recipes with my own appetite in mind as well as what my friends and *MyHalalKitchen.com* readers have asked for over the years. I hope you'll get as much satisfaction out of them as I do at home.

**IN THIS CHAPTER**

YIELD: 1¼ CUPS
SPECIAL EQUIPMENT: Whisk

# Korean Chili Sauce

*It's hard to find the words to describe how much I love this sauce. I not only use it in Asian cooking and to add to Asian foods, but I actually use it on anything in which I'm craving a little more heat; it's that good. No need for the bottled stuff, make batches of this sauce yourself and keep it in the fridge for all the dishes you'd like to spice up, too.*

½ cup + 1 tablespoon fresh chili paste

⅓ cup water

3 tablespoons sesame oil

3 teaspoons mild (light) honey

1   In a small mixing bowl, combine all the ingredients and whisk vigorously until well combined.

2   Transfer to an airtight container and store in the refrigerator for 2 to 3 months.

YIELD: 1¼ CUPS
SPECIAL EQUIPMENT: Whisk

# Sweet and Sour Sauce

*Most Americans are familiar with sweet and sour chicken, but you can use this sauce on beef, lamb, and fish, too.*

1 cup raw cane sugar

½ cup unseasoned rice vinegar

¼ cup ketchup

2 tablespoons Soy Sauce Alternative (recipe follows)

2 cloves garlic, minced

1   In a small mixing bowl, combine all the ingredients and whisk vigorously until well combined.

2   Transfer to an airtight container and store in the refrigerator for 2 to 3 months.

YIELD: ¾ CUP
SPECIAL EQUIPMENT: Whisk

# Teriyaki Sauce

*I make this popular Japanese sauce myself because it is often made with* mirin, *a sweet Japanese wine. The substitute I use gives the sauce just the right amount of sweetness, and the fruit juices help the sauce adhere to meat and other proteins when cooking.*

½ cup + 2 tablespoons white grape juice (not from concentrate)

¼ cup + 2 tablespoons Soy Sauce Alternative (recipe follows)

3 tablespoons honey

1 teaspoon minced fresh garlic

½ teaspoon ground ginger

1   In a small mixing bowl, combine the grape juice and Soy Sauce Alternative. Add the honey and whisk until well combined. Add the garlic and ginger and whisk until well combined.

2   Transfer to an airtight container and store in the refrigerator for 2 weeks.

YIELD: ¾ CUP
SPECIAL EQUIPMENT: Whisk

# Soy Sauce Alternative

*Soy sauce is widely available, so you may not see much reason to make it yourself. I came up with an alternative because naturally brewed soy sauce has remnants of alcohol in it, and alcohol-free versions often contain synthetic ingredients I'd rather not consume. I also like making it myself because I can control the salt, especially when most commercially available brands are really salty to my taste buds.*

¼ cup + 2 tablespoons molasses

3 tablespoons raw cane sugar

¼ teaspoon sea salt

¼ teaspoon ground cumin

⅛ teaspoon ground black pepper

⅔ cup water

3 tablespoons dark sesame oil

1   In a small mixing bowl, combine the molasses, sugar, and spices. Add the water and whisk until well combined. While whisking constantly, slowly drizzle in the oil.

2   Transfer to an airtight container and store in the refrigerator for 2 to 3 months.

# Hot and Sour Soup

*Hot and Sour Soup is a longtime favorite at American Chinese restaurants. It is sometimes made with chicken broth, which means many of those who observe a* dhabiha *halal diet might be inclined to skip it. By making it yourself, you can enjoy it in the comfort of your own home. I recommend enjoying a hot pot of green tea with this soup.*

1½ quarts Chicken Broth (see recipe on p. 32)

2 tablespoons minced ginger, plus more for garnish

3 teaspoons sea salt, or to taste

2 teaspoons raw cane sugar

½ teaspoon white pepper

1 tablespoon cornstarch dissolved in 1 tablespoon warm water

8 ounces soft tofu

½ cup chopped green onions, plus more for garnish

1 tablespoon rice vinegar

1 teaspoon red pepper flakes

3 whole large eggs, whisked

Soy Sauce Alternative (see recipe on p. 104), for serving

1   In a medium saucepan over high heat, bring the Chicken Broth to a boil.

2   In a small mixing bowl, combine the ginger, salt, sugar, and white pepper. Add the mixture to the saucepan and stir until combined. Add the cornstarch–water slurry to the saucepan and whisk vigorously until the slurry is completely dissolved.

3   Reduce the heat to medium–high and add the tofu, green onions, vinegar, and red pepper flakes to the saucepan.

4   While beating the whisked eggs with a fork simultaneously, slowly pour them into the saucepan. Simmer for 5 minutes. Remove from the heat.

5   Transfer to serving bowls and serve hot with the Soy Sauce Alternative and garnish with the ginger and green onions.

# Korean Beef Bulgogi

*This just might be my favorite Korean dish ever, but it's nearly impossible to find a halal restaurant that serves it. Its flavor is deep and complex, but the ingredients are quite simple and basic. Bulgogi is traditionally served wrapped in lettuce leaves, but it's delicious served with rice, too.*

1 pound beef cuts for stir fry-ing (skirt, hanger, brisket, or sirloin tip), thinly sliced

½ cup Soy Sauce Alternative (see recipe on p. 104)

¼ cup + 2 tablespoons rice vinegar

¼ cup + 2 tablespoons raw cane sugar

2 tablespoons minced garlic

2 tablespoons sesame seeds

¼ teaspoon sea salt

¼ teaspoon white pepper

1 tablespoon sesame oil

1 tablespoon sunflower oil

2 carrots, thinly sliced

1 cup thinly sliced green onions

8 leaves romaine lettuce, for serving

Korean Chili Sauce (see recipe on p. 103), for dipping (optional)

1  In a large mixing bowl, combine the beef, Soy Sauce Alternative, rice vinegar, sugar, garlic, sesame seeds, salt, and white pepper. Cover with plastic wrap and refrigerate for 30 minutes to 4 hours.

2  In a large sauté pan over medium heat, warm the oils. Add the meat (discarding the marinade) and cook on 1 side for 5 minutes, until browned. Turn and repeat until all sides are browned.

3  Add the carrots and green onions to the sauté pan and cook for 5 minutes. Remove from the heat.

4  Transfer to a platter or bowl and serve hot with the lettuce leaves and a side of the Korean Chili Sauce, if desired.

# Japanese Beef Teriyaki

*You can substitute chicken, lamb, shrimp, or a hearty white fish like walleye or cod for the beef in this recipe, if desired. If you have skewers, consider preparing this on the grill.*

¾ cup Teriyaki Sauce (see recipe on p. 104)

¼ teaspoon sea salt

¼ teaspoon white pepper

2 tablespoons sesame oil

2 tablespoons sunflower oil

1 pound beef cuts for stir frying (skirt, hanger, brisket, or sirloin tip), cut into ½-inch-thick slices

Cooked vegetables and steamed rice, for serving

Sesame seeds, for sprinkling (optional)

1  In a small mixing bowl, combine the Teriyaki Sauce, salt, and white pepper. Stir until well blended.

2  In a large sauté pan over medium heat, gently warm the oils. Add the meat and cook on 1 side for 5 minutes, until browned. Turn and repeat until all sides are browned.

3  Reduce the heat to low and add the Teriyaki Sauce mixture to the sauté pan. Cook, uncovered, for 10 minutes.

4  Transfer to a platter and serve hot with sides of vegetables and rice. Sprinkle with the sesame seeds, if desired.

YIELD: 4 SERVINGS
SPECIAL EQUIPMENT: Whisk

# Chinese Beef Pepper Steak

*Most Chinese restaurant menus include this classic dish. My recipe for pepper steak will be a favorite in your home, too. Don't skip the white pepper—it adds an authentic flavor you won't want to miss.*

1 tablespoon sesame oil, plus more if needed

1 tablespoon grape seed or sunflower oil, plus more if needed

1 pound beef cuts for stir frying (skirt, hanger, brisket, or sirloin tip), thinly sliced

2 tablespoons Soy Sauce Alternative (see recipe on p. 104)

2 tablespoons rice vinegar

3 cloves garlic, minced

1 tablespoon raw cane sugar

2 teaspoons freshly grated ginger

2 teaspoons sea salt

1 teaspoon freshly ground black pepper

1 teaspoon white pepper

2 tomatoes, quartered

1 green bell pepper, cored and thinly sliced

1 red bell pepper, cored and thinly sliced

1 tablespoon cornstarch or potato starch dissolved in ¼ cup lukewarm water

Sesame seeds, for sprinkling (optional)

Steamed rice, for serving

1   In a large sauté pan over medium heat, warm the oils. Add the meat and cook on 1 side for 5 minutes, until browned. Turn and repeat until all sides are browned.

2   In a small mixing bowl, combine the Soy Sauce Alternative, rice vinegar, garlic, sugar, ginger, salt, black pepper, and white pepper. Add the mixture to the pan. Remove the meat from the pan and transfer to a plate.

3   Add the tomatoes and peppers to the pan and stir to coat. Add more of the oils if needed. Cook for 5 minutes, until the peppers become tender.

4   Add the cornstarch–water slurry to the saucepan and whisk vigorously until the slurry is completely dissolved.

5   Return the meat to the pan. Add more sesame oil, if needed, and sauté for 5 to 7 minutes. Remove from the heat.

6   Transfer to a platter or bowl. Sprinkle with the sesame seeds, if desired. Serve hot with the rice.

**RESOURCES**

I use Otafuku Rice Vinegar.

YIELD: 4 SERVINGS
SPECIAL EQUIPMENT: Whisk

# Mongolian Stir Fry

*During my college days, I frequented a Mongolian stir-fry restaurant in Cleveland's Coventry Village neighborhood. I loved the huge variety offered there; you could build your own meal, but they added their own secret seasonings and sauces while cooking the meal before your eyes. Instead of lamb and the vegetables I've listed here, you can choose beef, fish, shrimp, or chicken and any type of vegetables you like with this dish.*

**For the Marinade**

¼ cup Soy Sauce Alternative (see recipe on p. 104)

¼ cup raw cane sugar

1 whole large egg, beaten

2 tablespoons minced garlic

1 tablespoon minced fresh ginger

2 teaspoons cornstarch

½ teaspoon baking soda

1 pound boneless lamb shoulder, thinly sliced

**For the Sauce**

¼ cup rice vinegar

¼ cup dark brown sugar

2 tablespoons Soy Sauce Alternative (see recipe on p. 104)

2 tablespoons honey

1½ tablespoons minced garlic

1 tablespoon sesame seeds

1 teaspoon Red Chili Sauce (see recipe on p. 185)

TO MAKE THE MARINADE

1  In a large mixing bowl, combine all the marinade ingredients and stir until well blended. Add the lamb to the bowl, toss until thoroughly coated, and cover with plastic wrap. Refrigerate for 1 hour to overnight.

TO MAKE THE SAUCE

1  In a small mixing bowl, combine all the sauce ingredients and whisk vigorously until well blended. Set aside.

TO MAKE THE SPICE MIX

1  In a separate small mixing bowl, combine all the spice mix ingredients and stir until well blended. Set aside.

TO PREPARE THE MEAT AND VEGETABLES

1  In a wok, cast-iron skillet, or large sauté pan over medium–high heat, warm 1 tablespoon each of the oils. Add the meat (discarding the marinade) and cook on 1 side for 2 minutes, until browned. Turn and repeat until all sides are browned. Transfer the meat to a paper towel–lined plate and scrape the bottom of the pan, loosening the fond formed by browning the meat.

**For the Spice Mix**

1 teaspoon pink Himalayan salt

½ teaspoon ground cinnamon

½ teaspoon ground fennel

½ teaspoon ground turmeric

¼ teaspoon white pepper

⅛ teaspoon ground cloves

⅛ teaspoon red pepper flakes

1 star anise (optional)

**For the Meat and Vegetables**

2 tablespoons sunflower oil, divided

2 tablespoons sesame oil, divided

4 green onions, thinly sliced

2 stalks celery, thinly sliced in 3-inch pieces

2 carrots, thinly sliced in 3-inch pieces

2 tablespoons chopped fresh cilantro leaves, for garnish

1 teaspoon sesame seeds, for garnish (optional)

Steamed rice, for serving

2  Add the remaining 1 tablespoon each of the sesame and sunflower oils and the vegetables to the pan and sauté for 2 to 3 minutes, scraping the bottom of the pan as you cook. Add the spice mix and stir until well blended.

3  Return the meat to the pan and add the sauce. Stir until well combined.

4  Reduce the heat to low, cover, and cook for 15 minutes. Remove from the heat.

5  Transfer to a platter and garnish with the cilantro leaves. Sprinkle on the sesame seeds, if using. Serve with the rice.

# Shrimp Pad Thai

*You know a dish is good when kids will eat it, right? I made this for a dear friend and her young sons once, and the kids loved it so much that my friend asked for the recipe. Score! There are peanuts in this dish, but if you're cooking for people with allergies, you can easily leave them out of the recipe.*

1 (14-ounce) package rice noodles

2 tablespoons sesame oil, divided

4 whole large eggs

¼ cup + 2 tablespoons rice vinegar

¼ cup raw cane sugar

¼ cup tamarind syrup

2 tablespoons Soy Sauce Alternative (see recipe on p. 104), plus more for dipping

1 teaspoon red pepper flakes

2 tablespoons vegetable oil

2 pounds raw shrimp, cleaned, deveined, and tails removed

3 cloves garlic, minced

2 tablespoons freshly grated ginger

2 teaspoons sea salt

½ teaspoon white pepper

¼ cup finely ground peanuts, divided

2 green onions, finely chopped, for garnish

2 tablespoons chopped fresh cilantro leaves, for garnish

Lime wedges, for garnish

Korean Chili Sauce (see recipe on p. 103), for dipping (optional)

1   In a medium mixing bowl, cover the rice noodles in warm water and soak for 20 to 30 minutes, until softened.

2   In a small sauté pan over medium heat, warm 1 tablespoon of the sesame oil. Add the eggs and cook, using a fork to fluff the eggs continuously, for 3 to 5 minutes, until the eggs are lightly scrambled. Remove from heat and set aside.

3   In a small mixing bowl, combine the rice vinegar, sugar, tamarind syrup, 2 tablespoons of Soy Sauce Alternative, and red pepper flakes.

4   In a deep-bottomed sauté pan over medium–high heat, heat the remaining 1 tablespoon of the sesame oil and the vegetable oil. Add the shrimp, garlic, ginger, salt, and white pepper and cook for 5 minutes, until the shrimp have turned bright pink.

5   Add the softened noodles and ½ of the peanuts to the pan. Continue cooking for 5 minutes, until all the liquid in the pan has cooked off. Add the eggs to the pan and stir until thoroughly combined. Remove from the heat.

6   Transfer the contents of the pan to a platter or individual plates. Garnish with the remaining peanuts, green onions, cilantro leaves, and lime wedges. Serve with the Soy Sauce Alternative on the side and the Korean Chili Sauce, if using.

# Sweet and Sour Chicken

*Everyone loves a good Sweet and Sour Chicken recipe; this one is my favorite. I store leftovers in Chinese take-out boxes with the rice in a separate box so they're fun and easy to reheat the next day, as the boxes keep everything tightly secured.*

1¾ pounds boneless skinless chicken breast, cut into cubes

½ cup cornstarch

2 whole extra large eggs

1 tablespoon water

⅓ cup sunflower or grape seed oil

¼ cup sesame oil

1¼ cups Sweet and Sour Sauce (see recipe on p. 103)

2 tablespoons sesame seeds, for sprinkling

¼ cup chopped green onions, for garnish

2 tablespoons minced fresh ginger, for garnish

Steamed rice, for serving

Soy Sauce Alternative (see recipe on p. 104), for dipping (optional)

Red Chili Sauce (see recipe on p. 185), for dipping (optional)

1   In a large mixing bowl, combine the chicken and the cornstarch. Ensure each piece is well coated.

2   In a shallow, wide bowl, combine the eggs and water. Using a whisk, beat until well combined.

3   Using tongs, dip 1 piece of the cornstarch-coated chicken into the egg–water mixture and then set the piece aside on a plate. Repeat until all the chicken has been dipped.

4   Preheat the oven to 350°F.

5   In a large oven-safe sauté pan or Dutch oven over low heat, warm the oils. Add the chicken and raise the heat to medium–high. Sauté for 2 to 3 minutes, until each piece is crispy on 1 side. Repeat until all sides are crispy. Remove from the heat and set aside to cool slightly.

6   Pour the Sweet and Sour Sauce over the chicken and stir until thoroughly coated. Cover the sauté pan, transfer to the oven, and bake for 15 minutes.

7   Remove the cover from the pan, turn each piece of chicken over, and bake, uncovered, for 15 minutes. Remove from the oven.

8   Transfer the chicken to a serving platter. Sprinkle with the sesame seeds. Garnish with the green onions and ginger and serve with the rice and the Soy Sauce Alternative and Red Chili Sauce, if desired.

# Coconut Balls

*If you're ever craving something sweet that has coconut in it or want to be taken momentarily to a tropical Asian locale, this recipe is for you. Ever since I've made them, the requests keep coming in to make more for parties and special events, so eventually I'll have to quadruple the recipe. In the meantime, it's just for our pleasure at home, and this recipe makes plenty to enjoy.*

4 cups finely shredded unsweetened dried coconut, divided

½ cup raw cane sugar

3 tablespoons unsalted butter, softened

½ cup heavy whipping cream

½ cup sweetened condensed milk

3 teaspoons Coconut Extract (see recipe on p. 54) or coconut emulsion

1 teaspoon all-natural food coloring (optional)

Butter, for greasing

1   In a medium saucepan, combine 3 cups of the shredded coconut, sugar, and butter. Stir until well combined. Add the cream, condensed milk, and Coconut Extract to the pan and stir until well combined. Place over low heat and cook, stirring constantly, for 10 minutes. (Cook for 15 minutes if not using food coloring and then remove from the heat and set aside to cool slightly.)

2   If using the food coloring, add to the saucepan and stir until all the color has been fully incorporated. Cook for 5 minutes. Remove from the heat and set aside to cool slightly.

3   Grease a 9-inch square baking dish with the butter. Pour the coconut mixture into the dish and level with a spatula. Cover with plastic wrap and refrigerate up to 4 hours or overnight.

4   Remove the baking dish from the refrigerator. Transfer the remaining 1 cup of shredded coconut to a wide, shallow bowl. Shape the chilled coconut mixture into 1- to 2-inch balls and then roll them in the shredded coconut until well coated. Set the coconut balls on a platter.

5   Serve immediately or refrigerate until serving.

# Mango Tapioca Pudding

*Many home cooks are unfamiliar with tapioca pearls, but they're a staple in Asian desserts and can be found in a variety of Asian markets such as Thai, Vietnamese, and Philippine grocery stores. If sealed properly the pearls last a very long time and can be used to make puddings like this and other delicious desserts, too.*

1¼ cups large tapioca pearls

1 cup water

1 cup raw cane sugar

2 (13½ ounce) cans coconut milk

2 ripe mangoes, diced

1 tablespoon cornstarch dissolved in 1 tablespoon warm water

1 tablespoon Orange Extract (see recipe on p. 56)

Pinch sea salt

1  In a medium mixing bowl, cover the tapioca pearls in cool water and soak for 20 minutes, until plump.

2  In a heavy-bottomed saucepan over medium–high heat, bring the 1 cup water to a boil. Add the sugar and stir until completely dissolved.

3  Add the tapioca pearls, coconut milk, diced mangoes, cornstarch–water slurry, Orange Extract, and salt to the saucepan. Stir vigorously as you cook for 3 to 5 minutes, until well combined. As soon as the mixture starts to get sticky and a little difficult to stir, remove from the heat.

4  Transfer the pudding into individual bowls. Refrigerate for 4 hours to overnight before serving.

**RESOURCES**

For coconut milk, I use Chaokoh brand; for tapioca pearls, I prefer those made by Golden Country Oriental Food.

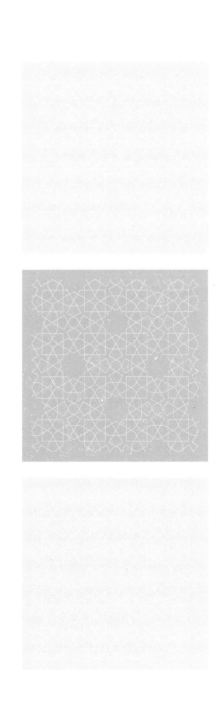

# CHAPTER 12

# French Cuisine

Next to the comforts of Italian home cooking, French food, especially the rustic kind, is my favorite. I make it regularly, now that I've found a great number of halal substitutes for the pork and alcohol. I love that I can incorporate seasonal produce from the Midwest, where I live, into many traditional French recipes, and embrace the same sort of passion the French have for maintaining and preserving their heritage, and all the culinary traditions that encompass simple cooking.

Making classical French cuisine halal might seem absolutely absurd to some people, but I challenge them to think outside the box. My alternatives don't inherently change the nature of the recipes but make the dishes accessible for people whose dietary requirements prevent them from enjoying the original classics. It's a way of opening up French cuisine (and all the other cuisines in this book) to a world of people who might not otherwise try them.

# Béchamel Sauce

*Béchamel Sauce is a French version of Italian Alfredo sauce without the Parmesan cheese. It's used in a wide variety of French dishes, and you'll find it is a key ingredient in my* Croque Monsieur *(see recipe on p. 128).*

4 tablespoons unsalted butter

2 cups whole milk

¼ cup all-purpose flour

¼ teaspoon sea salt, or to taste

⅛ teaspoon freshly ground black pepper, or to taste

1   In a small, deep-bottomed saucepan over medium heat, gently warm the butter. Add the milk and whisk until well combined. Cook for 3 minutes, until the milk has thoroughly warmed. While whisking vigorously, add the flour, 1 tablespoon at a time, until all has been added and the sauce is well combined.

2   Season with the salt and black pepper and remove from the heat. Serve or use immediately.

**VARIATION**

For a cheesy Béchamel Sauce, add 1 cup grated Gruyére cheese to the saucepan just after the flour has been completely incorporated. Note that some variations of Gruyére contain rennet from non-halal sources. Choose carefully.

YIELD: 1⅓ CUPS

SPECIAL EQUIPMENT: Whisk

# Béarnaise Sauce

*Growing up, I never knew Béarnaise was a French sauce. My mother liked to make what became my favorite French-inspired meal: breaded chicken with Béarnaise Sauce. But the sauce she made involved adding a packet of dried spices to melted butter in a saucepan. Once I realized how to make it from scratch, I've never gone back to the packets—and you don't have to, either. The white wine in the classic recipe is replaced here with a halal, no-alcohol substitute. Do not make the sauce ahead of time, as it tends to separate when reheated.*

⅓ cup white grape juice (not from concentrate)

2 tablespoons chopped fresh tarragon

2 tablespoons minced shallots

2 tablespoons white balsamic vinegar

¼ teaspoon sea salt

⅛ teaspoon freshly ground black pepper

3 egg yolks

3 sticks unsalted butter, melted and cooled to room temperature

1  In a large saucepan over medium heat, combine the grape juice, tarragon, shallots, vinegar, salt, pepper, and black pepper. Cook for 7 minutes, until the liquid has been reduced to only about 1 to 2 tablespoons in volume. Immediately remove from the heat and set aside.

2  In a separate bowl, vigorously whisk the egg yolks.

3  While whisking grape juice mixture constantly, add the beaten yolks to the large saucepan. Reduce the speed of your whisking and slowly add the melted, cooled butter to the large saucepan. Increase the speed of your whisking and continue to vigorously whisk the sauce until it thickens. Serve or use immediately.

YIELD: 1⅓ CUPS

SPECIAL EQUIPMENT: Immersion blender or whisk

# Hollandaise Sauce

*This bright yellow sauce is the highlight of my Eggs Benedict (see recipe on p. 71). It's easy to make, but it does need to be put together quickly, so make sure to prepare all the ingredients before you begin cooking.*

1½ sticks unsalted butter

4 egg yolks

2 tablespoons fresh lemon juice

⅛ teaspoon sea salt

⅛ teaspoon freshly ground black pepper

⅛ teaspoon cayenne pepper

1   In a small, deep-bottomed saucepan over low heat, gently warm the butter. Once it is melted, immediately remove from the heat.

2   In a deep mixing bowl, combine the remaining ingredients. Use an immersion blender or whisk vigorously to integrate the ingredients.

3   Slowly transfer the melted butter into the mixing bowl. Resume using the immersion blender or whisking vigorously until the sauce becomes rich and creamy.

# French Onion Soup with Gruyére Cheese
## (Soupe a l'Oignon au Fromage)

*I've always loved classic French Onion Soup, so when I began to eat a halal diet I experimented with a variety of quality grape juices that would be a suitable alternative for this dish. What I've found is that a high quality juice, not from concentrate, with a deep purple color and sweet taste works best for this dish, making this a delicious alternative way to make the soup.*

**4 tablespoons unsalted butter**

**2 tablespoons olive oil**

**4 cups thinly sliced yellow onions**

**2½ teaspoons sea salt**

**2 tablespoons flour**

**½ cup Concord grape juice (not from concentrate)**

**1 teaspoon raw cane sugar**

**1 quart Beef Broth (see recipe on p. 31)**

**½ loaf French bread, cut into 4–6 (1-inch) slices**

**2 cups freshly grated Gruyère cheese**

1  In a 4½-quart Dutch oven over medium heat, melt the butter. When the butter begins to froth, add the oil. Once the oil is warmed, add the onions and salt. Reduce the heat to medium–low and cook, stirring constantly, for 15 minutes, until the onions have softened and are well browned.

2  Add the flour to the Dutch oven and whisk or stir with a wooden spoon until the ingredients are well combined. Gently add the grape juice and sugar and mix well. Add the Beef Broth and stir to combine.

3  Set the oven to broil.

4  Raise the heat to medium–high and bring to a boil. Immediately reduce the heat to medium and simmer, covered, for 20 to 30 minutes.

5  During the last 5 minutes of the soup's cooking time, place the bread slices on a parchment-lined baking sheet. Scatter the cheese evenly over the slices of bread and place the baking sheet under the broiler. Broil for 3 minutes, until melted and browned. Remove from the oven.

6  Remove the soup from the heat and ladle it into bowls. Place a slice of the cheese bread on top of each bowl. Dunk the bread slightly into the soup.

**COOKS' NOTE**

If you have individual serving oven-safe bowls, you can fill them with the soup, place them on the parchment-lined baking sheet, and place the bread on top of each bowl. Scatter the cheese over each slice of bread and place the baking sheet directly under the broiler for 3 minutes.

# Mixed Salad with Poached Eggs and *"Lardons"*

*This is a great salad recipe for winter, because the dressing is served hot over the greens. With chopped breakfast beef strips standing in for the lardons (small strips of bacon or bacon fat), there's no loss of remaining fat to use in the delicious dressing that's made right in the same pan.*

1 tablespoon white vinegar

4 whole large eggs

Sea salt, to taste

Freshly ground black pepper, to taste

1 tablespoon unsalted butter

8 slices (about ½ pound) beef breakfast strips, diced

¼ cup minced yellow onion or shallots

2 teaspoons balsamic vinegar

2 teaspoons dry mustard powder

1 cup roughly chopped mixed salad greens (such as endive, Boston lettuce, romaine, or red leaf), washed and dried

1   In a deep-bottomed sauté pan over medium heat, bring 4 inches of water to a slow boil and then add the vinegar (it helps the eggs stay together in the water). Slowly add each egg, 1 at a time, to the boiling water. Reduce the heat to medium–low and season the eggs with the salt and pepper. Cover and cook for 4 to 5 minutes. Remove from the heat.

2   Using a spatula or slotted spoon, gently remove each egg from the water. Drain off any excess water and set aside.

3   In a cast-iron skillet or sauté pan over medium heat, warm the butter. Add the beef strips to the pan and cook for 3 to 5 minutes on each side. Remove from the heat. Transfer the beef strips to a paper towel–lined plate to drain any excess fat.

4   Return the skillet to medium heat and add the onion. Cook for 2 to 3 minutes, until the onion is softened and browned. Add the vinegar and mustard powder and stir until combined. Taste and add more salt and black pepper, if desired. Remove from the heat and set aside to cool slightly.

5   Evenly distribute the salad greens among 4 serving plates. Top each mound of greens with equal amounts of the beef strip pieces and a single poached egg. Pour the warm dressing over the egg on each plate and serve warm.

# Croque Monsieur

*This classic French sandwich typically contains ham or salami, so I've found a wonderful substitute that is easy to get at most halal meat shops and delis: smoked turkey. It's just the right texture to keep this sandwich hearty while holding up to the preparation process that makes it so incredibly delectable.*

**8 slices Country Bread (see recipe on p. 61)**

**16 slices smoked turkey, sliced thick**

**½ cup Béchamel Sauce (see recipe on p. 121)**

**2 cups freshly shredded Gruyére cheese**

**2 tablespoons unsalted butter**

1   Place 4 slices of the Country Bread on a parchment-lined baking sheet. Place 4 slices of the turkey on top of each piece of bread. Drizzle 2 tablespoons of the Béchamel Sauce over each of the piles of turkey and then sprinkle each with ¼ cup of the cheese on top. Place the remaining 4 slices of Country Bread on top of the cheese, making 4 sandwiches total.

2   Set the oven to broil.

3   In a large oven-safe sauté pan over medium–high heat, melt the butter. Place each sandwich in the pan and cook 2 to 3 minutes, until browned on 1 side. Turn the sandwich over and cook for 2 to 3 minutes, until browned on the other side. Transfer the sandwich to the prepared baking sheet. Repeat until all sandwiches have been toasted in the sauté pan. Remove from the heat.

4   Evenly sprinkle the remaining 1 cup of cheese over each of the sandwiches. Place the baking sheet in the oven and broil for 3 to 5 minutes, until the cheese on top has melted and slightly browned. Remove from the oven and set aside to cool slightly.

5   Slice each sandwich on the diagonal and serve immediately.

# Breaded Chicken with Béarnaise Sauce

*This is my favorite French-inspired recipe and is a favorite in our test kitchen. Best of all, it's a hit with adults and kids alike. Be sure to start the sauce only when the chicken is ready, as it will separate if it sits too long.*

**2 whole large eggs, beaten**

**1 tablespoon water**

**2 cups breadcrumbs**

**Pinch salt**

**Pinch freshly ground black pepper**

**4 boneless skinless chicken breasts, pounded thin**

**¼ cup olive or grape seed oil**

**1⅓ cups Béarnaise Sauce (see recipe on p. 122)**

**Blanched French green beans or other vegetables, for serving**

1   In a shallow, wide bowl, combine the eggs and water. Using a whisk, beat until well combined.

2   In a separate wide, shallow bowl, combine the breadcrumbs, salt, and black pepper and stir until well blended.

3   Using tongs, dip 1 piece of the chicken into the egg–water mixture and then the breadcrumb mixture. Shake off any loose breadcrumbs and set the piece aside on a plate. Repeat until all the chicken has been coated in breadcrumbs.

4   In a large oven-safe sauté pan or Dutch oven over low heat, warm the oil. Add the chicken and raise the heat to medium–high. Sauté for 5 to 7 minutes, until each piece is browned on 1 side. Turn over and sauté for 5 to 7 minutes, until browned on the other side. For the last 5 minutes of cooking, cover the pan in order to ensure the chicken is thoroughly cooked. Remove from the heat.

5   Transfer the chicken breasts to a platter. Place the Béarnaise Sauce in a pourable container. Serve the chicken breasts alongside the Béarnaise Sauce and the green beans.

# Beouf Bourguignon with a Red Wine Substitute

*This is the quintessential French dish that Julia Child was famous for making. As a home cook, I couldn't do without this recipe in my repertoire. My halal substitute for Burgundy wine gives the dish a deep color and perfect sweetness. Beef broth is a must in this recipe, adding extra richness, so don't skip it.*

⅓ cup diced beef breakfast strips

2 pounds sirloin steak, cut into 1½-inch cubes

2¼ teaspoons sea salt

1 teaspoon freshly ground black pepper

2 tablespoons olive oil

8 small Yukon gold potatoes, halved

2¼ cups peeled and roughly chopped carrots

½ cup finely diced yellow or white onion

3 cloves garlic, minced

1 tablespoon tomato paste

Several sprigs fresh thyme

3 bay leaves, crushed

1 quart Beef Broth (see recipe on p. 31)

2 cups Concord grape juice (not from concentrate)

2 tablespoons unsalted butter

½ pound mushrooms, chopped in half

1 loaf crusty French bread, for serving

1   In a large, deep-bottomed, oven-safe saucepan or Dutch oven over medium heat, sauté the beef strips in their own fat for 3 minutes, until they are nicely browned and somewhat crisp.

2   Add the steak cubes to the saucepan and season with the salt and black pepper. Cook on 1 side for 5 minutes, until browned. Turn and repeat until all sides are browned. Transfer the meat to a paper towel–lined plate and scrape the bottom of the saucepan, loosening the fond formed by browning the meat.

3   Preheat the oven to 325°F.

4   Add the oil to the saucepan. Add the potatoes and carrots and cook, stirring constantly to avoid sticking, for 5 minutes, until the vegetables are well browned.

5   Add the onion, garlic, tomato paste, thyme sprigs, and bay leaves to the saucepan and stir until thoroughly combined.

6   Raise the heat to medium–high and add the Beef Broth and grape juice to the saucepan. Bring to a boil. Reduce the heat to medium and simmer, uncovered for 10 minutes. Remove from the heat.

7   Cover the saucepan and place in the oven for 2½ hours.

8   During the last 30 minutes of cooking time, melt the butter in a small sauté pan over medium heat. Add the mushrooms and sauté for 10 to 12 minutes, until the mushrooms are well browned. Remove from the heat and set aside.

9   Remove the saucepan from the oven. Uncover and gently stir in the sautéed mushrooms. Return the saucepan to medium–high heat and cook for 30 minutes. Remove from the heat.

10  Serve hot with the crusty French bread.

YIELD: 4 SERVINGS
SPECIAL EQUIPMENT: Whisk

# Coq without the Vin

*The classic French poultry dish coq au vin (chicken in wine) is traditionally made not just with wine but also bacon. Made with some simple halal alternatives, my version is just as tasty as the original. A roux is a thickener made by combining fat (in this case, butter) and flour. A roux gives a dish a wonderful texture; this recipe wouldn't be the same without it.*

**3 ounces beef breakfast strips (about 6 slices)**

**1 whole chicken, cut up, skin removed, and patted dry**

**1½ teaspoons sea salt, plus more to taste if desired**

**½ teaspoon freshly ground black pepper, plus more to taste if desired**

**2 cups Concord grape juice (not from concentrate)**

**2 tablespoons minced garlic**

**1 tablespoon tomato paste**

**2 sprigs fresh or 2 teaspoons dried thyme**

**2 bay leaves**

**4 tablespoons unsalted butter, divided**

**1 pound crimini or button mushrooms, roughly chopped**

**½ yellow onion, thinly sliced**

**3 tablespoons all-purpose flour**

**1 (1-pound) package pappardelle or egg noodles, cooked**

**2 tablespoons chopped fresh flat leaf parsley, for garnish**

1   In a large, deep-bottomed saucepan or Dutch oven over medium heat, sauté the beef strips in their own fat for 3 minutes, until they are nicely browned and somewhat crisp. Remove the strips to a paper towel–lined plate to drain any excess fat.

2   Season each of the chicken pieces with the salt and black pepper. Add the chicken pieces to the saucepan and cook on 1 side for 5 minutes, until browned. Turn and repeat until all sides are browned.

3   Return the beef strips to the saucepan. Add the grape juice, garlic, tomato paste, thyme, and bay leaves. Cover and cook over medium heat for 25 minutes.

4   While the chicken is cooking, in a large sauté pan over medium–high heat, melt 2 tablespoons of the butter. Add the mushrooms and onion. Season to taste with the salt and pepper and sauté for 10 minutes, until the mushrooms are browned and the onion is translucent and browned.

5   Create a roux by combining the remaining 2 tablespoons of butter and the flour in a small mixing bowl. Mix them together with your fingers until the butter and flour are fully incorporated.

6   Remove the cover from the saucepan. Using a slotted spoon, remove the chicken pieces from the saucepan and set them aside on a plate. Remove and discard the bay leaves. Add the roux to the saucepan and whisk vigorously until the roux has completely integrated into the liquid, the mixture has thickened, and there are no lumps. Return the chicken to the saucepan and gently stir in the sautéed mushrooms and onion.

7   Raise the heat to medium–high and bring the mixture to a boil.

8   Reduce the heat to medium, cover, and simmer for 20 minutes. The liquid in the saucepan should be thick enough to slightly stick to the back of a spoon. (If not, raise the heat to high and cook, uncovered, for 2 to 3 minutes, until the sauce cooks down.) Remove from the heat.

9   Remove the chicken with a slotted spoon and transfer to a serving platter lined with the cooked pappardelle or egg noodles. Ladle the sauce, including the mushrooms and onion, over the chicken and pasta. Garnish with the parsley and serve hot.

# Bouillabaisse
## (Provençal Fish Stew)

¼ cup olive oil

½ cup diced yellow onion

2 cups roughly chopped tomatoes

3 cloves garlic, minced

2 tablespoons tomato paste

1 cup white grape juice (not from concentrate)

1 tablespoon freshly grated orange zest

2 teaspoons sea salt

1 teaspoon dried thyme

1 teaspoon freshly ground black pepper

1 quart fish broth or water

3 lobster claws, cleaned and rinsed (optional)

1 pound cod, cleaned, rinsed, and cut into bite-size chunks

½ pound mussels in their shells, cleaned and rinsed

½ pound raw shrimp, cleaned, rinsed, deveined, and tails removed

½ cup chopped fresh flat leaf parsley

½ teaspoon red pepper flakes (optional)

Rustic French bread, for serving

*The aromas of this stew remind me of summer visits to Sicily during my childhood. The air of my family's seaside village was filled with the aromas of fish and seafood dishes. I've recreated these fragrances at home often, especially in the summer, in an attempt to recapture my memories of that enchanted isle. This delicious stew is one of my favorites. White grape juice, my choice of halal substitute, really helps bring the dish together and takes me back to the Mediterranean with every bite. If you prefer it, you can use a more flavorful grape juice, such as Concord.*

1  In a large stockpot over medium heat, warm the oil. Add the onion and sauté for 2 to 3 minutes, until translucent.

2  Add the tomatoes and garlic to the stockpot and cook for 3 to 5 minutes, until the tomatoes are softened. Stir in the tomato paste.

3  Raise the heat to medium–high and add the grape juice, orange zest, salt, thyme, and black pepper to the stockpot. Add the fish broth and bring to a boil.

4  Reduce the heat to medium and add the lobster claws, if using, cod, mussels, and shrimp to the stockpot. Cover and cook for 20 minutes.

5  Add the parsley and red pepper flakes, if using, and cook, uncovered, for 10 minutes. Remove from the heat.

6  Ladle stew into large soup bowls. Serve hot with rustic French bread, for dunking.

YIELD: 4½ CUPS
SPECIAL EQUIPMENT: Whisk

# Berry Hot Sipping Chocolate

*I've read many French recipes in which wine was added to hot chocolate. Instead, I use a halal substitute that adds sweet fruit flavor and is perfect for a very cold winter night.*

**12 ounces frozen mixed berries (strawberries, blueberries, and raspberries)**

**2 tablespoons raw cane sugar**

**¼ cup Concord grape juice (not from concentrate)**

**8 ounces dark chocolate, broken into small pieces**

**2 tablespoons unsweetened Dutch cocoa powder**

**2½ cups whole milk**

**Cocoa nibs, for topping (optional)**

**¼ cup fresh berries, for topping (optional)**

**1 sprig fresh mint, for topping (optional)**

1   In a medium saucepan over high heat, combine the berries and sugar. Cook, stirring constantly, for 3 to 5 minutes, until the fruit is warmed and the sugar has melted.

2   Add the grape juice to the saucepan and mash the fruit with the back of a spoon or a potato masher. Cook, stirring constantly, for 5 minutes, until the mixture is smooth.

3   Add the chocolate and cocoa powder to the saucepan and stir until melted. Add the milk and whisk until all ingredients are thoroughly combined. Cook, stirring constantly, for 3 to 5 minutes. Remove from the heat.

4   Serve hot in small coffee cups or mugs topped with the cocoa nibs, fresh berries, and mint, if desired.

**RESOURCES**

I buy Askinosie Chocolate Roasted Cocoa Nibs and Frontier Co-Op Fair Trade Cocoa Powder.

YIELD: 24 COOKIES

SPECIAL EQUIPMENT: Cooling rack, 2 madeleine baking pans, stand mixer fitted with the whisk attachment or whisk

# Orange Madeleines

*My mom has been making madeleines for family gatherings for years. Many of my family members wondered how she could make the cookies look just like clamshells. I knew my Francophile mother's secret—a madeleine pan. Today, it's one of the many baking utensils she owns that I don't, and to test this citrus-flavored madeleine recipe, I had to borrow her pan several times. My family loves these cookies, and I hope you will, too. If you don't have a madeleine pan and don't want to buy one, find someone who does and ask if you can borrow it. In return, you can share some of the cookies you make with it!*

3 whole large eggs

½ cup raw cane sugar

2 teaspoons Orange Extract (see recipe on p. 56)

1 teaspoon orange blossom water

1 cup unbleached all-purpose flour, plus more for dusting

½ teaspoon baking powder

Freshly grated zest of 1 orange (about 1 teaspoon)

¼ cup unsalted butter, melted and cooled

Confectioners' sugar, for dusting

1  Preheat the oven to 400°F.

2  In the bowl of a stand mixer fitted with the whisk attachment, beat together the wet ingredients—the eggs, sugar, Orange Extract, and orange blossom water—for 1 minute, until the mixture is well combined and has thickened. Turn off the mixer. (You can also use a hand whisk.)

3  In a medium mixing bowl, combine the dry ingredients—the flour, baking powder, and zest. Stir until well combined.

4  Add the dry ingredient mixture into the bowl of the stand mixer in thirds, beating at low speed for 2 to 3 minutes, until just combined and the mixture has no lumps. Add the melted butter and continue beating for 2 minutes, until the mixture is well combined. Turn off the mixer.

5   Grease 2 madeleine baking pans and dust them with flour.

6   Using a spoon or an ice cream scoop containing about 1 table-spoon of the batter, fill each madeleine shell in the pan halfway. Bake for 11 to 12 minutes. Remove from the oven.

7   Release each madeleine from the pan and place it on a cooling rack, flat side down. Set aside for 1 hour, until cooled to room temperature.

8   Sprinkle the madeleines with the confectioners' sugar and transfer to a platter. Serve.

# Simmered Pears

*If you've never had this dish, you're missing out on one of the world's most delicious and elegant dessert recipes. These simmered pears are traditionally cooked in wine, but I use a sweet cherry juice and get the same beautiful, delicious results. It's a lovely centerpiece for a small dinner party, as it perfectly serves a party of four.*

2 cups sweet cherry juice

½ cup dark honey

Freshly squeezed juice and freshly grated zest of 1 lemon

2 cinnamon sticks

1 star anise

4 Bartlett or Anjou pears, peeled but stems left intact

Fresh Table Cream (see recipe on p. 38) or crème fraîche, for serving (optional)

1. In a small, deep saucepan over medium–high heat, combine the cherry juice, honey, lemon juice and zest, cinnamon sticks, and star anise and bring to a boil.

2. Reduce the heat to medium and add the pears to the saucepan. Simmer for 40 minutes, ladling the juice over the pears from time to time as they cook. Remove from the heat.

3. Transfer the pears to individual serving bowls. Ladle the juice over the pears and serve warm, with the Fresh Table Cream, if using.

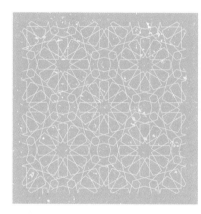

# CHAPTER 13

# Italian Cuisine

ITALIAN CUISINE WILL ALWAYS BE my ultimate comfort food and the heart and soul of my kitchen. I grew up on Sicilian flavors, of course, but through my extensive travels throughout Italy, I've come to know much of the country's diverse cuisine. From the most northern region of Lake Como to the very southern Sicilian town of Ragusa, I've had the pleasure of enjoying it all—dishes that are hearty or light, tomato-based or creamy, vegetarian or thoroughly meaty, but always superbly fresh. There is no other cuisine on the planet that delights me more, particularly when bread, cheese, olive oil, tomatoes, and basil are involved—the essentials I couldn't live without.

To make traditional Northern Italian dishes halal, substitutes are often necessary; many of them include alcohol and pork. The Italian food I grew up on was truly Mediterranean—heavy on the seafood, light on the meat, so I really enjoyed the challenge of figuring out how to make the Northern Italian specialties that are included in this chapter halal.

YIELD: 8 SERVINGS

# Italian Wedding Soup

*Italian Wedding Soup is a hearty soup made with chicken, vege-tables, and mini-meatballs. Many meatball recipes combine beef with pork, so I've recreated my family's recipe in a halal way that preserves the wonderful taste of the soup my mother and grand-mother used to make. Since there are so many ingredients and the recipe cooks quickly, it's best to gather all the ingredients before cooking. Be sure there's enough room in your refrigerator to ac-commodate a baking sheet loaded with mini-meatballs.*

¼ cup olive oil

3 carrots, diced

½ yellow onion, diced

4 cloves garlic, minced

1 whole chicken, cut up, skin removed, and patted dry

1½ teaspoons + ¼ teaspoon sea salt, divided

½ teaspoon + ⅛ teaspoon freshly ground black pep-per, divided

2½ quarts Chicken Broth (see recipe on p. 32)

1 pound ground beef

½ cup breadcrumbs, finely processed

⅓ cup freshly grated Parme-san cheese, plus more for sprinkling if desired

1 whole large egg, slightly beaten

¼ cup chopped fresh curly or flat leaf parsley

2 cups water

4 cups frozen or fresh spinach

½ pound dried orzo or other small pasta

1  In a large Dutch oven over medium–high heat, warm the oil. Com-bine the carrots, onion, and garlic and sauté for 2 to 3 minutes.

2  Season the chicken with the 1½ teaspoons salt and ½ teaspoon black pepper and add it to the Dutch oven. Cook on 1 side for 5 to 7 minutes, until browned. Turn and cook for 5 to 7 minutes, until browned on the other side. Add the Chicken Broth and bring to a boil.

3  Reduce the heat to medium. Cover and cook for 30 minutes.

4  Line a baking sheet with parchment paper.

5  In a large mixing bowl, combine the ground beef, breadcrumbs, Parmesan cheese, egg, parsley, remaining ¼ teaspoon salt, and remaining ⅛ teaspoon black pepper. Using your hands, gently mix the ingredients until just combined.

6  Using your hands, roll a generous tablespoon of the mixture into a 1-inch ball. (Work quickly, as you need to keep the meat cold enough to retain its shape.) Repeat until all the meatballs are formed. Place each mini-meatball on the prepared baking sheet and store the mini-meatballs in the refrigerator.

7   Once the chicken has cooked in the soup for 30 minutes, add the chilled mini-meatballs, 1 at a time, to the Dutch oven. Add the water to the Dutch oven and bring the soup to a boil.

8   Partially cover the Dutch oven, reduce the heat to medium, and cook for 1½ hours.

9   Uncover the Dutch oven and, using tongs, gently remove the chicken and set aside on a plate to cool. Add the spinach and pasta to the soup and continue to cook for 5 to 7 minutes.

10  Once the chicken has cooled, remove the meat from the bones and discard the bones. Add the meat to the soup and stir until well combined. Cover and cook for 5 to 10 minutes to warm the chicken.

11  Ladle into soup bowls and sprinkle with the additional Parmesan cheese, if desired.

**COOKS' NOTE**

If you choose to refrigerate the soup before serving and reheating, remember that the noodles will plump up quite a bit. You may want to add more Chicken Broth or water before heating it up again.

# Antipasto Platter

*At most of the Sicilian family gatherings I attended during my childhood, we'd enjoy beautiful antipasto platters. Antipasto, Italian for "before the meal," is an appetizer that features an assortment of deli meats, olives, peppers, and cheeses. You can find many of the halal deli meats I describe below at most Mediterranean and Middle Eastern markets around the country. The steps below describe a traditional arrangement of an antipasto platter; see the photo at left for a more contemporary presentation.*

¼–½ pound each thinly sliced beef mortadella with pistachio, beef salami, turkey salami, smoked turkey, oven-roasted turkey, and roast beef

1½ cups mixed olives (Kalamata, green, and cured black Moroccan)

½ cup cubed Parmesan cheese

½ cup cubed Fontina cheese

½ cup pepperoncini (pickled hot peppers)

Lemon slices, for garnish

½ cup capers

1   On a large platter, arrange the deli meats in rows, keeping the same kind in each row.

2   Arrange the olives in rows according to type and do the same with the cheese.

3   Decorate the platter with the pepperoncini and garnish with the lemon slices. Sprinkle the meat with the capers.

4   Serve with small forks and/or toothpicks to allow your guests to help themselves.

# Meatball Sandwiches

*Before I adopted a halal diet, this was always a favorite for me at Italian restaurants and sandwich shops. For a long time, I could only look at it longingly on menus, but now, I make it myself! Be sure to prepare the sauce first, so once the meatballs are made, they can be added to the warm sauce and begin cooking immediately.*

**For the Tomato Sauce
(YIELDS 1½ QUARTS
[24 OUNCES])**

¼ cup olive oil, plus 2 table-spoons for finishing

1 yellow or white onion, minced

½ teaspoon sea salt

2 (14½-ounce) cans plum tomatoes, unsalted and crushed

3 cups tomato sauce

½ cup tomato paste

¼ cup raw cane sugar

1 tablespoon dried parsley

1 tablespoon dried oregano

2 leaves fresh basil, chopped

## TO MAKE THE TOMATO SAUCE

1  In a large, deep-bottomed saucepan over medium heat, warm the ¼ cup of oil. Add the onion and salt and sauté for 2 to 3 minutes, until translucent.

2  Add the plum tomatoes, tomato sauce, tomato paste, sugar, parsley, oregano, and basil. Using an immersion blender, purée the sauce as it cooks. Slowly raise the heat to medium–high and simmer for 20 minutes.

## TO MAKE THE MEATBALLS

1  In a large mixing bowl, combine the ground beef, onion, garlic, breadcrumbs, egg, Parmesan and Romano cheeses, parsley, oregano, salt, and black pepper. Using your hands, gently mix the ingredients until just combined.

2  Using your hands, roll a medium-size piece of the mixture into a 2½-inch ball. As you finish rolling each meatball, place it on a cutting board.

**For the Meatballs**

1 pound ground beef
(80% lean, 20% fat)

1 small yellow or white onion,
finely grated

2 large cloves garlic, finely
grated

½ cup breadcrumbs

1 whole large egg, slightly
beaten

¼ cup freshly grated
Parmesan cheese

¼ cup freshly grated Romano
cheese

2 tablespoons chopped fresh
or 1 tablespoon dried curly
parsley

2 tablespoons chopped fresh
or 1 tablespoon dried
oregano

¼ teaspoon sea salt

⅛ teaspoon freshly ground
black pepper

**For the Sandwiches**

6 hoagie rolls, toasted

1 cup freshly grated Parmesan
cheese, for sprinkling

½ pound sliced fresh mozzarella cheese, for topping

¼ cup chopped fresh curly
parsley, for garnish

TO FINISH THE SANDWICHES

1  After the sauce has simmered for 20 minutes and is piping hot, add the meatballs to the saucepan.

2  Raise the heat to high and bring to a boil. Quickly reduce the heat to medium and add the remaining 2 tablespoons of oil to the sauce. Partially cover the saucepan and simmer for 3 hours. Remove from the heat.

3  Ladle some sauce on each toasted hoagie roll and then add a few meatballs to each. Sprinkle evenly with the Parmesan and top with the mozzarella cheese. Garnish with the parsley. (If you prefer the cheese melted, simply place each sandwich in a toaster oven for 1 to 2 minutes.) Serve hot.

YIELD: 4–6 SERVINGS

# Mediterranean Shrimp Scampi

*This is by far the most requested recipe by my readers. Chefs love it, too, because most shrimp scampi recipes call for white wine, and chefs often need to substitute for wine for a variety of dietary needs. I find that a simple, all-natural, not-from-concentrate white grape juice makes a perfectly delicious substitute. It gives the dish a subtle sweet flavor that beautifully complements the cooked garlic and fresh tomatoes.*

**6 cloves garlic, chopped into large pieces**

**1 stick unsalted butter**

**1 tablespoon olive oil**

**2 large tomatoes, diced**

**½ small white onion, diced**

**2 pounds fresh shrimp, cleaned thoroughly**

**¼ cup white grape juice (not from concentrate)**

**½ teaspoon sea salt, or to taste**

**¼ teaspoon freshly ground black pepper, or to taste**

**1 (1-pound) package capellini or angel hair pasta, cooked and drizzled with olive oil to prevent sticking**

**2 tablespoons freshly grated Romano cheese, for sprinkling**

**2 tablespoons chopped fresh flat leaf parsley, for garnish**

1  In a small saucepan over very low heat, combine the garlic and butter and cook for 10 minutes, until the garlic has softened. Remove from the heat and set aside.

2  In a large, deep skillet over medium–high heat, warm the oil. Add the tomatoes and sauté for 2 to 3 minutes, until they have softened. Add the onion and sauté for 2 to 3 minutes, until it is translucent.

3  Add the shrimp to the skillet and cook for 3 to 5 minutes on 1 side, until they begin to turn pink. Turn and cook for 3 to 5 minutes on the other side.

4  At this point, the liquid in the skillet should have cooked down to some degree. Add the grape juice and reduce the heat to medium. Cook for 1 to 2 minutes.

5  Add the garlic–butter mixture to the skillet and stir until well combined. Season with the salt and pepper.

6  Add the cooked pasta to the skillet and remove from the heat. Using tongs or 2 large forks, integrate the sauce and shrimp into the noodles. Taste and season further with the salt and pepper, if desired.

7  Transfer to a large serving bowl. Sprinkle with the Romano cheese and garnish with the parsley. Serve hot.

YIELD: 4 SERVINGS

SPECIAL EQUIPMENT: Immersion blender

# Penne without the Vodka

*Penne alla vodka is now a very popular Italian dish, but I don't recall it from my childhood. I'm always up to try something new, but since vodka certainly isn't halal, I figured I'd better come up with my own recipe. This is creamy and delicious.*

3–5 tablespoons olive oil, divided

½ cup chopped yellow onion

4 cloves garlic, crushed

1 (14½-ounce) can plum tomatoes, unsalted and crushed

⅓ cup tomato sauce

⅓ cup white grape juice (not from concentrate)

2 tablespoons raw cane sugar

½ teaspoon sea salt, plus more to taste if desired

½ cup heavy whipping cream

1 (1-pound) package penne pasta, cooked and drizzled with olive oil to prevent sticking

½ cup shredded mozzarella cheese, for topping

2 tablespoons chopped basil, for garnish

1 tablespoon red pepper flakes

1 In a large, deep saucepan over medium heat, warm 2 to 4 tablespoons of the oil. Add the onion and garlic and sauté for 2 to 3 minutes, until softened.

2 Add the plum tomatoes, tomato sauce, grape juice, sugar, and salt. Using an immersion blender, purée the sauce as it cooks.

3 Add the heavy cream and simmer for 20 minutes. Remove from the heat.

4 Place the remaining 1 tablespoon of oil in the bottom of a large pasta serving bowl. Add some of the pasta to the bowl and the a few ladles of the sauce. Continue layering the pasta and sauce into the bowl until all has been transferred to the serving bowl. Using tongs or 2 large forks, integrate the sauce into the pasta. Taste and season further with the salt. Continue to toss until well combined.

5 Top with the mozzarella cheese and garnish with the basil. Season with the red pepper flakes and serve hot.

# Lasagna with Meat Sauce

*Sunday dinners at my Sicilian grandparents' home almost always featured lasagna with meat sauce. Many Italian recipes mix ground beef and pork in their meat sauces, so it's a good idea to make it yourself to be sure the meal is halal. As you'll see, this recipe is not that hard to do, and just about everyone who tries it loves it.*

**For the Meat Sauce**

2 tablespoons olive oil, plus more if needed

2 pounds ground beef

1 white onion, minced

3 cloves garlic, minced

1½ teaspoons dried parsley

1½ teaspoons dried oregano

1 teaspoon sea salt

½ teaspoon freshly ground black pepper

2 recipes (yields 3 quarts [48 ounces]) Tomato Sauce (see the Meatball Sandwiches recipe on p. 150)

### TO MAKE THE MEAT SAUCE

1   In a large sauté pan over medium heat, warm the oil. Add the ground beef and cook, stirring constantly, for 5 minutes, until browned. Drain the fat and return to the heat.

2   Add the onion, garlic, parsley, oregano, salt, and black pepper to the sauté pan and cook for 10 minutes. (If the meat begins to dry out, consider adding a little more oil.) Remove from the heat and transfer the cooked ground beef into the Tomato Sauce. Set aside.

### TO MAKE THE FILLING

1   In a large mixing bowl, combine the ricotta, mozzarella, cream, parsley, salt, and black pepper. (The consistency should be pourable, but not runny.) Set aside until ready to use.

**For the Filling**

**2 pounds Ricotta Cheese (see recipe on p. 37)**

**2 cups shredded mozzarella cheese**

**¼ cup heavy cream**

**¼ cup chopped fresh curly parsley**

**1 teaspoon sea salt**

**½ teaspoon freshly ground black pepper**

**To Assemble the Lasagna**

**2 (1-pound) packages no-boil lasagna noodles**

**½ pound fresh mozzarella cheese, sliced thin**

**1 cup shredded mozzarella cheese**

**¼ cup chopped fresh basil leaves**

**¼ cup chopped fresh curly parsley**

TO ASSEMBLE THE LASAGNA

1   In the bottom of a 9-inch × 13-inch baking dish, place about 2 cups of the Meat Sauce. Place 1 row of the lasagna noodles on top of the sauce. Next, add 1 layer of the filling.

2   Repeat the layering process (Meat Sauce, then noodles, then filling) until all of each has been used. Preheat the oven to 375°F.

3   Set the assembled lasagna aside at room temperature for 30 minutes to allow the noodles to soften.

4   Cover the top layer of the lasagna with a mixture of the fresh and shredded mozzarella cheese. Tent the dish with foil and bake for 35 minutes.

5   Remove the foil tent from the dish and bake for 7 minutes.

6   Add the basil and parsley and bake for 3 minutes. Remove from the oven and set aside on a wire rack to cool for 10 to 15 minutes.

7   Slice and serve hot.

# Linguine with Mussels

*Although this is a Southern Italian dish, it's also very popular in the South of France. Be sure to get your mussels from a reputable fishmonger and clean them well before cooking.*

4 tablespoons unsalted butter, divided

2 tablespoons olive oil

1 cup diced fresh tomatoes

¼ cup minced garlic

1 teaspoon sea salt, plus more to taste if desired

1 cup diced yellow onion

2 cups white grape juice (not from concentrate) or 1 cup white grape juice + 1 cup fish broth

1½ pounds mussels in their shells, cleaned and rinsed

1 (1-pound) package linguine pasta, cooked and drizzled with olive oil to prevent sticking

½ cup freshly grated Parmesan cheese, for sprinkling

½ cup chopped fresh flat leaf parsley, for garnish

1. In a large, deep saucepan over medium heat, warm 2 tablespoons of the butter and the oil. Add the tomatoes, garlic, and salt and sauté for 3 minutes. Add the onion and sauté for 3 minutes.

2. Add the grape juice, or grape juice–fish broth mixture, and tomato paste and stir until well combined. Add the mussels, cover, and cook for 10 to 12 minutes, until the mussels' shells are open. (Remove and discard any mussels whose shells do not open.)

3. Add the cooked pasta and the remaining 2 tablespoons of butter to the saucepan. Using tongs or 2 large forks, integrate the sauce into the pasta. Taste and season further with the salt if needed. Continue to toss until well combined. Remove from the heat.

4. Transfer the contents of the saucepan to a large platter. Sprinkle with the Parmesan cheese and garnish with the parsley. Serve hot.

# Spaghetti Carbonara

*One of my all-time favorite Italian comfort-food recipes can now be made at home just like it's made at some of the best Italian restaurants—just with beef instead of the traditional pancetta.*

1 tablespoon olive oil

12 ounces smoked beef breakfast strips

⅓ cup diced onion

4 whole large eggs

1½ teaspoons whole milk

1 teaspoon salt, plus more to taste if desired

½ teaspoon freshly ground black pepper, plus more to taste if desired

1 cup heavy whipping cream

1 (1-pound) package spaghetti, cooked and drizzled with olive oil to prevent sticking

1½ cups freshly grated Parmesan cheese, divided

¼ cup chopped fresh curly parsley, for garnish

1   In a large, deep-bottomed sauté pan over medium heat, warm the oil. Add the beef strips to the pan and cook for 5 minutes on each side, until the strips have begun to brown.

2   Add the onion to the sauté pan and cook for 2 to 3 minutes, until the onion is softened and browned.

3   In a small mixing bowl, combine the eggs, milk, salt, and black pepper. Whisk vigorously until very well combined and thickened (so the eggs will not scramble upon transfer to the hot sauté pan).

4   Slowly add the egg mixture to the sauté pan. Quickly add the cream to the pan and whisk until the mixture is thoroughly combined.

5   Add the cooked spaghetti and ¾ cup of the Parmesan cheese to the sauté pan and remove from the heat. Using tongs or 2 large forks, integrate the sauce and cheese into the spaghetti. Taste and season further with the salt and pepper, if desired.

6   Transfer to a serving platter. Sprinkle with the remaining ¾ cup of the Parmesan cheese and garnish with the parsley. Serve hot.

YIELD: 4 SERVINGS
SPECIAL EQUIPMENT: Whisk

# Chicken Florentine

*If you like creamy dishes, you'll love this one. It's easy enough to prepare for a weeknight dinner but also elegant enough to serve at a small dinner party. My halal substitute for white wine tastes great and adds a hint of sweetness to the sauce in this recipe.*

**4 boneless skinless chicken breasts**

**¾ cup + 2 tablespoons all-purpose flour, divided**

**½ teaspoon sea salt, plus more to taste if desired**

**½ teaspoon freshly ground black pepper, plus more to taste if desired**

**4 tablespoons unsalted butter**

**½ cup white grape juice (not from concentrate)**

**4 cloves garlic, minced**

**12 ounces fresh spinach**

**½ cup diced yellow onion**

**2 cups half and half**

**½ cup freshly grated Parmesan cheese, for sprinkling**

**Cooked pasta or crusty Italian bread, for serving**

1   Place the chicken breasts on a sheet of plastic wrap and then cover them with a second sheet of plastic wrap. Using a heavy object, such as a meat tenderizer, pound the chicken breasts to about a ⅛-inch thickness, until they are nearly translucent.

2   In a wide, shallow bowl, combine the ¾ cup of flour, the salt, and the black pepper and stir until well blended. Using tongs, dip 1 piece of the chicken into the flour mixture. Shake off any loose flour and set the piece aside on a plate. Repeat until all the chicken has been coated in flour.

3   In a large deep-bottomed sauté pan over medium–high heat, melt the butter. Once the butter begins to froth, add the chicken. Sauté for 5 minutes, until each piece is browned on 1 side. Turn over and sauté for 5 minutes, until browned on the other side.

4   While the chicken is browning, in a medium saucepan over low heat, combine the grape juice and garlic. Once it becomes warm, add the spinach. Cover and cook for 5 minutes, until the spinach has wilted. Remove from the heat, drain of all liquids, and set aside.

5   Once the chicken is browned, transfer it to a plate and immediately add the onion to the sauté pan. Sauté over low heat for 10 minutes, until the onion is translucent and lightly browned.

6  Add the half and half to the sauté pan and then vigorously whisk in the remaining 2 tablespoons flour. Season further with the salt and black pepper, if desired.

7  Once the sauce begins to thicken, add the contents of the saucepan and the chicken to the sauté pan. Cover and cook for 7 to 10 minutes.

8  Transfer to a platter, sprinkle with the cheese, and serve with the cooked pasta or crusty Italian bread.

# Spaghetti Bolognese with Pappardelle Pasta

*This is a pretty hearty spaghetti dish and can be made with ground beef, as suggested here, or turkey, if you like it a little leaner. Both are great substitutes for pork.*

¼ cup + 1 tablespoon olive oil, divided

½ cup diced yellow onion

2 stalks celery, diced

2 carrots, minced

4 cloves garlic, minced

1½ teaspoons sea salt, plus more to taste if desired

1 teaspoon freshly ground black pepper

1 pound ground beef

½ teaspoon thyme

2 bay leaves

⅓ cup tomato paste

1½ cups Concord grape juice (not from concentrate)

2 (8-ounce) packages pappardelle pasta, cooked and drizzled with olive oil to prevent sticking

½ cup freshly grated Parmesan cheese, for sprinkling

1   In a medium saucepan over medium heat, warm the ¼ cup of oil. Add the onion, celery, carrots, and garlic and sauté for 5 minutes, until browned. Season with the salt and black pepper.

2   Add the ground beef, thyme, and bay leaves to the saucepan and cook for 5 to 7 minutes, until the ground beef is browned.

3   Add the tomato paste and stir until well combined. Add the grape juice and reduce the heat to low. Cover and cook for 20 minutes. Remove from the heat. Remove and discard the bay leaves.

4   Place the remaining 1 tablespoon of oil in the bottom of a large pasta serving bowl. Add some of the pasta to the bowl and a few ladles of the Bolognese sauce. Continue layering the pasta and sauce into the bowl until all has been transferred to the serving bowl. Using tongs or 2 large forks, integrate the sauce into the pasta. Taste and season further with the salt if needed. Continue to toss until well combined.

5   Sprinkle with the Parmesan cheese. Serve hot.

# Chocolate Zabaglione

*This is the Italian version of chocolate mousse. To me, it tastes like a cross between pudding and mousse, with a silky texture you just can't find in storebought puddings. My halal substitute for the wine in the traditional recipe lends just the right amount of sweetness.*

1⅓ cups heavy whipping cream

6 egg yolks

¼ cup raw cane sugar

¼ cup roughly chopped pistachios

8½ ounces semi-sweet chocolate

1 tablespoon unsalted butter

1 teaspoon Vanilla Extract (see recipe on p. 56)

1 teaspoon Concord grape juice (not from concentrate)

Whipped cream, for topping

1   In a blender, combine the cream, egg yolks, sugar, and pistachios. Purée for 45 seconds to 1 minute, until thoroughly combined and mostly smooth.

2   In a medium saucepan over medium–low heat, combine the chocolate, butter, Vanilla Extract, and grape juice. While whisking constantly to prevent the chocolate from burning, cook for 3 to 5 minutes, until the chocolate has melted. Remove from the heat.

3   While continuing to whisk constantly, slowly add the contents of the blender to the saucepan. Continue whisking until the mixture is smooth and fully combined and the texture has thickened.

4   Transfer the mixture into small ramekins or sundae glasses, each about ¾ full. Refrigerate for 1 hour.

5   Top each serving with the whipped cream and serve cold.

# Lemon Tiramisù

*Tiramisù is one of the very first Italian recipes I converted to a halal preparation. The traditional recipe includes rum and often include gelatin. This version veers from classic tiramisù flavors but has fun, zesty twists—lemon flavor and edible yellow sugar pearls, which you can find at most craft stores and many bakeries.*

1 cup Mascarpone Cheese (see recipe on p. 36)

¼ cup heavy whipping cream, plus more if desired

2 tablespoons crème fraîche or Fresh Table Cream (see recipe on p. 38)

2 tablespoons raw cane sugar

3 teaspoons Lemon Extract (see recipe on p. 55)

Freshly grated zest of 3 lemons, plus more for sprinkling

2 cups cold dark-roast coffee or espresso

16 ladyfinger cookies (often known as *savoiardi*)

1–2 tablespoons edible lemon sugar pearls, for sprinkling

**RESOURCES**

I buy ladyfingers by Fomo Bonomi or Trader Joe's; for espresso, I choose Lavazza or Café Bustelo; and for lemon sugar pearls, I buy the Wilton brand.

1   In a large mixing bowl, combine the Mascarpone Cheese, cream, crème fraîche, sugar, Lemon Extract, and lemon zest and stir until well combined. The mixture should have the consistency of pourable cream; if not, add more cream or even some whole milk, ½ teaspoon at a time.

2   Spread ⅓ of the Mascarpone Cheese mixture on the bottom of a deep 9-inch square glass baking dish and smooth it out with a spatula.

3   Place the coffee in a wide, shallow bowl. Transfer 8 of the ladyfinger cookies to the bowl containing the coffee and allow them to soak for 6 to 10 seconds, until they have absorbed some of the coffee but are still firm enough to sit flat in the baking dish.

4   Place the soaked ladyfingers on top of the layer of Mascarpone Cheese mixture in the baking dish. Add another ⅓ of the Mascarpone Cheese mixture on top of the ladyfingers and smooth it again.

5   Soak the remaining ladyfinger cookies in the bowl containing the coffee for the same period of time. As before, place them on top of the Mascarpone Cheese mixture in the baking dish and coat them with the remaining ⅓ of the Mascarpone Cheese mixture.

6   Sprinkle the top layer of the dish with the lemon zest and sugar pearls. Cover the dish with plastic wrap and refrigerate for at least 1 hour to overnight, to allow it to set.

7   Slice and serve chilled, either on small plates or in small cups.

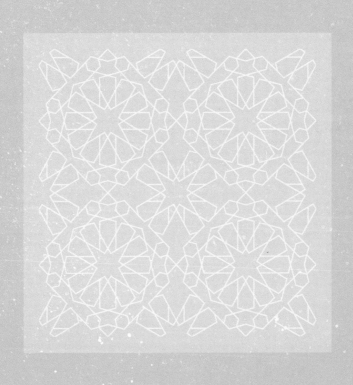

# CHAPTER 14

# Latin Cuisine

I WAS SLOW TO EMBRACE LATIN CUISINE because growing up, I didn't have it that often. My *abuela* (grandmother) lived in Puerto Rico, but when she visited us, she'd always bring packages of goodies from her hometown, Orocovis—guava and coconut candies, fresh mangoes, and, most important of all, homemade *pasteles*. Similar to Mexican tamales, these pasteles were a gelled concoction of meat and garbanzo beans wrapped in banana leaves. The flavors were similar to those of *arroz con pollo y gandules,* or rice with chicken and beans, and both delicious and comforting. Everything she brought smelled like what I imagined the island to be: fragrant, spicy, and tropical.

Years later, I had the chance to travel abroad in Spain and in Puerto Rico, Mexico, and Belize. Only then did I really understand the diversity of Latin cuisine. While studying Spanish in the quaint town of Segovia, Spain, and living just down the street from the castle where Queen Isabella was crowned, I ate regional paella cooked over an open fire in the countryside, enjoyed fried potato and onion tapas, and delighted in the creamiest desserts I've ever had.

As I continued my studies in the Yucatán town of Mérida, Mexico, I traveled extensively throughout the country and was completely taken aback by the diversity of Mexican cuisine. For example, I tried fresh shark meat in

**IN THIS CHAPTER**

*ceviche* in Playa del Carmen, lamb tacos in an off-the-beaten-path restaurant outside of Guadalajara, and tacos made with lake-caught fish. In the jungle of Palenque, I had tropical fish tamales made by local indigenous women. Then, my journeys led me to Belize, where I tasted my way through small towns.

As I developed my own cooking style and learned more about global cuisine, I discovered just how frequently pork products were used throughout the Latin world. I took it as a challenge to preserve the flavors I cherished in a halal way.

The best experience of all was teaching myself how to make *pasteles* using boiled *yautia* and plantains, just like my grandmother did. My mom and I sourced all the ingredients from a Caribbean market in Cleveland and made them for my *abuelo* (grandfather), who gave his full approval of their authenticity—even though we used chicken broth instead of lard. The memory is all the more special because at the end of his life's journey, he was able to see his granddaughter—me—embrace and create our traditional food with passion and love. Sadly, it would be the last time he had those foods, but we cherish that he delighted in their creation as much as he enjoyed eating them.

Overall, I've come to deeply respect and enjoy the diversity of Latin cuisine. This chapter's recipes are particularly near and dear to my heart, because each one is attached to a fond memory of a person or place that helped me become the cook I am today. I turn to these recipes again and again because they are delicious and satisfying, made with halal ingredients that leave me no excuse not to make them, and help preserve a heritage that deserves to be shared.

YIELD: 2 TABLESPOONS
SPECIAL EQUIPMENT: Spice grinder or mortar and pestle

# *Achiote* Seasoning

*Achiote, or annatto, is a reddish condiment that hails from the annatto tree. It is commonly used in Latin cooking to tint rice an orange-reddish color. It's also used commercially for the same reason. Find it Latin or Philippine markets or in the Hispanic aisle of an international grocery store.*

1 tablespoon ground annatto (*achiote*) seed (can usually be found at Hispanic or Philippine markets)

1 tablespoon whole coriander seeds

1   Using a spice grinder or a mortar and pestle, grind together the annatto and coriander seeds until the mixture is very fine. Store in an airtight container and keep in a cool place if grinding for later use.

YIELD: 1½ CUPS

# *Adobo*

*Adobo is a Latin spice mixture. Used in combination with vinegar and olive oil, it becomes a marinade that gives meats a distinctly Latin flavor.*

5 cloves garlic, minced

1 cup roughly chopped yellow onion

½ cup extra virgin olive oil

2 tablespoons white vinegar

2 teaspoons dried oregano

½ teaspoon sea salt, or to taste

½ teaspoon freshly ground black pepper, or to taste

1   In a large mixing bowl, combine all the ingredients. Stir until very well combined and set aside at room temperature until ready to use.

YIELD: 2 CUPS

SPECIAL EQUIPMENT: Food processor fitted with the "S" blade or blender

# Sofrito

*This sauce base gives dishes a quintessential Latin flavor.*

**1 green bell pepper, cored and roughly chopped**

**1 small yellow onion, roughly chopped**

**1 bunch cilantro, roughly chopped**

**3–4 cloves garlic, roughly chopped**

**1 serrano pepper, seeds and stem removed**

**1 tomato, roughly chopped**

**1 teaspoon ground cumin**

1   In the bowl of a food processor fitted with the "S" blade or a blender, combine all the ingredients. Pulse or purée until the ingredients are thoroughly combined and the *Sofrito* is very smooth.

2 pounds boneless skinless chicken thighs

¼ cup minced + 1 whole clove garlic, divided

¼ cup olive oil, divided

2 tablespoons dried oregano

2 tablespoons fresh chopped curly parsley

1 teaspoon sea salt, plus more to taste if desired

1 teaspoon red pepper flakes

1 teaspoon freshly ground black pepper, plus more to taste if desired

1 cup minced onion

⅔ cup freshly squeezed orange juice (about 2 oranges)

⅓ cup freshly squeezed lime juice (about 2 limes)

2 bay leaves

2½ cups Chicken Broth (see recipe on p. 32)

1 garlic clove

1 tablespoon unsalted butter

8 slices bread

¼ cup yellow mustard

8 slices Swiss cheese

8 thin slices smoked turkey

1 cup sliced pickles

# Cuban Sandwiches

*It's been a very long time since I've had a traditional Cuban sandwich—since way back when, during a trip to Miami and Key West. On the trip, I stopped at as many Cuban restaurants as I could find. Cubans revere the authenticity of this sandwich—always featuring ham and pork shoulder—so I've created a version with halal meats for anyone who misses this sandwich style and wants to have it without the pork.*

1 In a large mixing bowl, combine the chicken, the minced garlic, 2 tablespoons of the oil, the oregano, the parsley, the salt, the red pepper flakes, and the black pepper. Stir and set aside.

2 In a large Dutch oven over medium heat, warm the remaining 2 tablespoons of oil. Add the onion and sauté for 3 to 5 minutes, until translucent. Add the marinated chicken, orange and lime juices, and bay leaves and cook for about 10 minutes.

3 Raise the heat to medium–high, add the Chicken Broth, and bring to a boil.

4 Reduce the heat to medium–low, cover, and cook for 2 hours. Remove from the heat. Remove and discard the bay leaves. Set aside to cool to room temperature.

5 In a small glass mixing bowl, combine the garlic clove and the butter. Place in the microwave and heat on high for 30 seconds. (You can also warm these together for 1 to 2 minutes over medium heat in a small saucepan.) Set aside.

6 Spread the garlic butter on 1 side of each slice of the bread. On a hot grill or in a toaster oven, toast the buttered slices. Repeat until all the bread has been toasted.

7   Spread the mustard on each slice of the toasted bread. Add 1 piece of the cheese to each slice. On top of the cheese, add a layer of the cooled chicken and then season with the salt and black pepper. Add a slice of turkey and season again with the salt and black pepper. Evenly divide the pickles among the stacks and then close each sandwich.

8   Place a large cast-iron pan or grill over medium–high heat. Place the sandwiches in the pan and place a foil-wrapped brick or similar heavy, flat object over each sandwich. Grill for 2 to 4 minutes, until the bread becomes crispy. Turn over each sandwich and repeat on the other side. Remove from the heat.

9   Transfer the sandwiches to individual serving plates and serve hot.

# Shredded Goat Tacos

*Young goat meat, known as* chivo *in Spanish, is a delicacy commonly found in Mexican cuisine. I see it on restaurant menus all the time. Goat is not as meaty as lamb, but when spiced and cooked well, it's absolutely delicious—especially on tacos.*

1–2 tablespoons extra virgin olive oil

1½ pounds goat shoulder, sliced into 1½-inch cubes

1 Vidalia or yellow onion, thinly sliced

1 green bell pepper, cored and thinly sliced

3 roma tomatoes, roughly chopped

3 roasted or raw cloves garlic, roughly chopped

1 teaspoon ground cinnamon

½ tablespoon red pepper flakes

½ tablespoon ground cumin

½ teaspoon crushed dried epazote (optional)

2 cups water

8 corn tortillas, warmed, for serving

Sliced fresh radish, salsa, sour cream, sliced avocado, chopped cilantro, minced onion, and hot sauce, for serving

1   In a large sauté pan over medium heat, warm the oil. Add the meat and cook on 1 side for 5 minutes, until browned. Turn and repeat until all sides are browned.

2   Add the onion and pepper to the sauté pan and sauté for 5 minutes, until both are softened. Add the tomatoes, garlic, cinnamon, red pepper flakes, cumin, and epazote, if using. Stir and cook for 1 to 2 minutes.

3   Raise the heat to medium–high and add the water. Bring to a boil. Immediately reduce the heat to low, cover, and cook for 2 to 3 hours, until the meat is easily shredded with a fork. Remove from the heat.

4   Transfer the meat and a little of the cooking liquid to a serving bowl and, using 2 forks, shred it. Serve hot with the warmed tortillas and the radish, salsa, sour cream, avocado, cilantro, onion, and hot sauce on the side.

# Slow-Cooked Lamb *Carnitas*

*When most people hear* carnitas, *which translates into English as "little meat," they usually think of pork. This is my go-to entertaining recipe when I'm in the mood for Mexican food. Guests love the way the lamb pulls right off the bone and stays so moist. In particular, this makes really awesome tacos. Who says the only way to make* carnitas *is with pork?*

8 cloves garlic, crushed

2 tablespoons olive oil

1 tablespoon dried oregano

1 tablespoon ground cumin

2 teaspoons ground coriander

2 teaspoons sea salt

1 teaspoon chili powder

4 pounds bone-in lamb shoulder (or 3½ pounds boneless)

¼ cup grape seed oil

2 cups diced onions

1 large whole jalapeño pepper

⅓ cup freshly squeezed orange juice (1–2 oranges)

⅓ cup freshly squeezed lime juice (2 large limes)

2 cups Lamb Broth (see recipe on p. 33)

8 corn tortillas, warmed, for serving

Sliced fresh radish, salsa, sour cream, sliced avocado, chopped cilantro, minced onion, and hot sauce, for serving

1   In a large mixing bowl, combine the garlic, olive oil, oregano, cumin, coriander, salt, and chili powder. Stir until well combined. Add the lamb to the bowl and rub the mixture into the meat.

2   In a large sauté pan or Dutch oven over medium heat, warm the grape seed oil. Add the onions and sauté for 2 to 3 minutes, until translucent.

3   Add the meat and cook on 1 side for 5 minutes, until browned. Turn the meat over and repeat until all sides are browned. Add the jalapeño pepper and the orange and lime juices and cook for 3 to 5 minutes.

4   Raise the heat to medium–high and add the Lamb Broth. Bring to a boil. Transfer to a slow cooker set on low or keep in the Dutch oven and reduce the heat to low. In the slow cooker, cook for 12 hours; on the stovetop, cook for 3 hours.

5   Once the meat is fully cooked and is easy to pull apart, remove from the heat. Using 2 forks, shred the meat. Remove and discard the bones.

6   Transfer the meat and the cooking liquid to a serving bowl. Serve hot with the warmed tortillas and the radish, salsa, sour cream, avocado, cilantro, onion, and hot sauce on the side.

YIELD: 4–6 SERVINGS

SPECIAL EQUIPMENT: Stand mixer fitted with the sausage-making attachment

# Beef *Chorizo*

*When most people hear the word* chorizo, *they think of ground pork or a Mexican-style pork sausage. I'm here to tell you that* chorizo *can be made with beef, too. My recipe is entirely from scratch; I even get the beef casings from my local butcher. Your butcher probably has them, too. They usually come in 5-foot-long strips, a perfect amount for 2 pounds of ground meat, but they can last indefinitely if they remain packed in salt.*

**2 pounds ground beef (80% lean, 20% fat)**

**2 tablespoons sea salt**

**2 tablespoons *Achiote* Seasoning (see recipe on p. 170)**

**1 tablespoon apple cider vinegar**

**1 tablespoon minced garlic**

**1 tablespoon fresh minced onion**

**1 tablespoon smoked paprika**

**1½ teaspoons ground cumin**

**1 teaspoon dark brown sugar or *piloncillo***

**½ teaspoon ground red pepper flakes or cayenne pepper**

**¼ teaspoon freshly ground black pepper**

**1 (5-foot) strip beef casing**

**2–3 tablespoons vegetable oil, plus more for cooking**

**Scrambled eggs or *Arroz Blanco* (see recipe on p. 181) and *Habichuelas* (see recipe on p. 180), for serving**

1   In a large mixing bowl, combine the beef, salt, *Achiote* Seasoning, apple cider vinegar, garlic, onion, paprika, cumin, brown sugar, red pepper flakes, and black pepper. Using your hands, gently mix the ingredients until just combined. Refrigerate for 3 hours to overnight.

2   Thoroughly rinse the beef casing to remove all the salt. Prepare the stand mixer with the sausage-making attachment and place a bowl to catch the sausages as they push through the casings. Affix the sausage casing to the attachment, pushing forward as much of the casing as possible and tying the end of the casing so that no meat will fall out of the end.

3   Add the oil to the spiced beef mixture, using your hands to gently mix it in.

4   Start the mixer on low speed. Place the spiced meat mixture in the receptacle and guide it through the casing. Once the casing is filled, find a spot every few inches to twist the casing, making individual sausages. Using a nonserrated knife, prick the casing of each sausage at least twice to prevent bubbling when they are cooked.

5    Either wrap the sausages in parchment paper and plastic wrap and store in the refrigerator or freezer or cook immediately. To cook the sausages, place a very small amount of oil in a cast-iron pan, sauté pan, or griddle over medium–high heat. Cook for 5 minutes on each side, until all juices run clear and the sausages are nicely browned. Remove from the heat.

6    Thinly slice the sausages and serve with the scrambled eggs or the *Arroz Blanco* and *Habichuelas*.

# *Carne Guisada*
# (Caribbean Beef Stew)

*This is a Puerto Rican dish inspired by the island's fusion of Caribbean and Spanish flavors. Serve with recipes that follow for* Habichuelas *(pinto beans),* Arroz Blanco *(white rice) and* Plátanos Fritos *(fried plantains).*

**2½ pounds beef stew meat, cut into 1½-inch cubes, rinsed and dried**

**1½ cups *Adobo* (see recipe on p. 170)**

**1 tablespoon olive oil, plus more if needed**

**2 cups halved or quartered Yukon gold potatoes**

**1 green bell pepper, cored and diced**

**½ cup diced yellow onion**

**3 cloves garlic, minced**

**¾ cup canned tomato sauce**

**3 teaspoons sea salt, or to taste**

**⅛ teaspoon freshly ground black pepper**

**2 cups Beef Broth (see recipe on p. 31)**

**2 cups *Sofrito* (see recipe on p. 171)**

**2 tablespoons *Achiote* Seasoning (see recipe on p. 170)**

**1 cup manzanillo olives**

**½ cup capers**

***Arroz Blanco* (see recipe on p. 181), *Habichuelas* (see recipe on p. 180), and *Plátanos Fritos* (see recipe on p. 183), for serving**

1   In a large mixing bowl, combine the meat and *Adobo*. Mix well, rubbing the spices into the meat. Set aside for 20 minutes.

2   In a large, deep-bottomed pan or Dutch oven over medium heat, gently warm the oil. Add the meat to the pan and cook on 1 side for 5 minutes, until browned. Turn the cubes and repeat until all sides are browned. Using a slotted spoon, transfer the meat to a plate lined with paper towels.

3   Add the potatoes to the pan and sauté for 5 minutes, until well-browned (add more oil if necessary). Add the bell pepper, onion, and garlic and sauté, stirring constantly, for 3 to 5 minutes, until the peppers have softened.

4   Add the tomato sauce, salt, and black pepper to the pan and cook, stirring often to prevent sticking, for 5 minutes.

5   Add the Beef Broth, *Sofrito*, and *Achiote* Seasoning to the pan and stir until combined. Reduce the heat to medium–low and return meat to the pan. Cover and cook for 45 minutes.

6   Add the olives and capers to the pan and cook, covered, for 1 to 1½ hours. Remove from the heat and set aside to rest for 10 minutes.

7   Remove the meat from the pan. Using 2 forks, shred the meat and transfer it to a serving bowl filled with the *Arroz Blanco*. Drizzle the sauce from the pan over the meat and rice.

8   Serve hot with the *Habichuelas* and *Plátanos Fritos*.

# *Habichuelas*
## (Pinto Beans)

*Pinto beans, which are also known as* habichuelas, *are commonly served as a side with Caribbean dishes.* Habichuelas *are sometimes cooked in lard, or pork fat. This recipe provides a very simple halal substitute by using olive oil, but you can also use vegetable or grape seed oil if you prefer to make it with a more neutral flavor.*

**1 tablespoon olive oil**

**3 tablespoons diced onion**

**5½ cups cooked pinto beans**

**1 tablespoon *Achiote* Seasoning (see recipe on p. 170)**

**1 teaspoon salt, or to taste**

**2 cups canned tomato sauce**

**½ cup *Sofrito* (see recipe on p. 171)**

***Arroz Blanco* (see recipe on p. 181), for serving**

1   In a medium saucepan over medium heat, gently warm the oil. Add the onion and sauté for 2 to 3 minutes, until it is nicely browned and translucent.

2   Add the cooked pinto beans, *Achiote* Seasoning, and salt to the saucepan and stir until well combined. Add the tomato sauce and the *Sofrito* and bring to a boil.

3   Immediately reduce the heat to low and cook for 45 minutes to 1 hour. Remove from the heat.

4   Transfer to a serving bowl and serve with the *Arroz Blanco*.

# *Arroz Blanco*
# (White Rice)

*If it's a Latin meal, rice has to be on the plate. There is no magic formula for making it, and most rice brands have directions for cooking right on the label. This recipe fits the amount to serve with the* Carne Guisada *recipe.*

1 quart water

¼ cup olive oil

2 cups medium-grain rice

2 teaspoons sea salt

1   In a medium saucepan over medium heat, bring the water to a boil. Add the oil.

2   Add the rice and the salt. Reduce the heat to low and cook, covered, for 20 minutes. Remove from the heat and remove the lid.

3   Fluff the rice with a fork. Replace the lid halfway, allowing the steam to release but keeping the rice warm until serving.

**VARIATION**

*Arroz Amarillo* **(Yellow Rice):** In a small saucepan over medium heat, gently warm 2 tablespoons of annatto seeds in the ¼ cup of olive oil to be used in the above recipe for 3 minutes. Strain out and discard the seeds and then use the oil as directed in the recipe.

# *Plátanos Fritos*
## (Fried Plantains)

*Fried plantains, or* Plátanos Fritos, *are served with Caribbean dishes as you might serve chips. Sometimes, they're smashed while ripe, salted, and fried and sometimes even smashed and fried again. I like them crispy on the outside and soft in the middle, so I fry only once. Either way, they're a delicious sweet and savory complement to my* Carne Guisada.

**3 ripe plantains**

**½ teaspoon sea salt, or to taste**

**1–2 tablespoons olive oil**

1   Thickly slice the plantains on a diagonal (about 5 slices per plantain) and season the slices with the salt.

2   In a sauté pan over medium heat, gently warm the oil.

3   Add the plantain slices and raise the heat to medium–high. Cook for 3 to 4 minutes, until browned on 1 side. Turn them over and cook for 3 to 4 minutes, until browned on the other side. Using a slotted spoon, transfer the plantain slices to a plate lined with paper towels. Remove from the heat.

4   Serve hot.

# Chicken Tamales in Red Chili Sauce

*Tamales are celebration food for many Mexican families. However, we found out that the* masa *(corn dough) necessary to make tamales was often prepared with lard. My halal alternative involves using my homemade Chicken Broth; it congeals the* masa *nicely and makes great-tasting tamales. You can substitute shredded beef, turkey, or even duck meat in this recipe. You should be able to find all the ingredients at a Latin market or in the Hispanic aisle of an international supermarket.*

**For the Corn Husks**

**24–48 dried corn husks, depending on how much you wish to stuff the tamales**

**For the Chicken**

**1 pound boneless chicken breast or thigh meat (or a combination of both)**

**Sea salt, as needed**

**Freshly ground black pepper, as needed**

### TO MAKE THE CORN HUSKS

1 Rinse each corn husk under cool water, scrubbing off any dirt. Place them in a large stockpot filled with cool water for 20 minutes.

2 Remove the husks from the water and set aside to air dry on a dish rack or on clean towels.

### TO MAKE THE CHICKEN

1 In a large stockpot over medium–high heat, combine the chicken and enough water to cover it. Season the water as desired (if using seasonings here, you may wish to reduce the amounts of salt you add in later steps). Bring to a boil and cook for 35 minutes, until the chicken is fully cooked and shreds easily with a fork. Remove from the heat.

2 Remove the cooked chicken to a strainer to drain. Discard the cooking water.

3 Using 2 forks, shred the meat into small pieces. Place the chicken in a 9-inch × 13-inch glass baking dish and set aside.

**For the Red Chili Sauce**
**(YIELD: 2 CUPS SAUCE)**

5 dried guajillo chili peppers

5 dried morita or chipotle chili peppers

3 dried ancho chili peppers

1 cup Chicken Broth (see recipe on p. 32), chilled

½ cup diced yellow onion

3 cloves garlic

1 tablespoon ground cumin

1 tablespoon sea salt

2 tablespoons olive oil

2 tablespoons whole-wheat flour

**For the *Masa***

1 cup Chicken Broth (see recipe on p. 32)

8 cups *masa seca* or dry *masa* (be sure its label indicates that it is for tamales)

2 teaspoons sea salt

1 teaspoon baking powder

2 tablespoons olive oil

## TO MAKE THE RED CHILI SAUCE

1. Place a large saucepan over medium–high heat and fill it ⅔ full of water. Bring to a boil. Add the chili peppers, reduce the heat to medium, and cook for 20 minutes, until the peppers are soft and the stems are easy to remove. Remove from the heat and drain the peppers into a colander. Set aside to cool.

2. Wearing gloves, remove the stems from the peppers. Slice each pepper lengthwise and remove all or some of the seeds (depending on how hot you wish the sauce to be). Discard the stems and seeds.

3. In a blender, combine the peppers, Chicken Broth, onion, garlic, cumin, and salt. Purée for 1 to 2 minutes. Set aside.

4. In a medium saucepan over medium heat, warm the oil. Add the flour and whisk vigorously, forming a paste. Reduce the heat to low and quickly add the blended chili mixture. Cook, whisking occasionally, for 5 to 7 minutes, until the sauce is smooth and free of lumps. Remove from the heat and set aside to cool for 30 minutes.

5. Pour all but ¼ cup of the cooled Red Chili Sauce over the chicken and stir until thoroughly combined. Reserve the remaining sauce.

## TO MAKE THE *MASA*

1. In a small saucepan over low heat, gently warm the broth.

2. In the bowl of a stand mixer fitted with the paddle attachment, combine the *masa seca*, salt, and baking powder. Add the warmed Chicken Broth and the oil and blend on medium speed for 1 to 2 minutes. Scrape down the sides and bottom of the stand mixer bowl to prevent lumps from forming. Blend for an additional minute on medium speed.

3. Examine the texture of the *masa* by working it with your hands. It should be a fine balance between wet and dry, and it should be easy to manipulate without falling apart in your hands. If it is too dry, add a little more oil; if it is too wet, add a little more *masa seca*. Set aside.

### TO ASSEMBLE THE TAMALES

1  Arrange the ingredients from left to right: the corn husks, the *masa*, and the chicken in the Red Chili Sauce.

2  Pull a thin strip vertically from 1 corn husk to use as a tie for each tamale. Do this to each of the husks to have enough ties to wrap all of the bundled tamales.

3  Arrange a single corn husk vertically in front of you, inside facing up.

4  Using a spoon or your clean hands, scoop ¼ cup of the *masa* and spread it horizontally along the middle portion of the corn husk. It should not be a thick layer, and it should not come too close to the edges.

5  Next, place 2 tablespoons of the shredded chicken mixture on top of the *masa* in a vertical position in the center of the husk. Bring each of the sides of the husks to the middle and bring the bottom portion of the husk upward to fold in half. Use 1 of the corn husk ties to wrap it tight.

6  Continue this process with all of the ingredients until all of the corn husks have been used. (Some chicken may remain.)

7  Place a large tamale pot or stockpot with a steamer insert and a lid containing 3 inches of water over medium–high heat and bring to a boil. Place the tamales standing up (with the closed part facing down) in the steamer insert.

8  Cover and steam for 2½ hours, until the *masa* is completely cooked and neatly pulls away from the corn husks, periodically checking the water level of the pot. Remove from the heat.

9  Remove the tamales from the steamer and open each husk. Remove the tamales from the husks and discard the husks.

10 Transfer the tamales to a platter and serve.

# Seafood, Chicken, and *Chorizo* Paella

*The first time I ever had this dish was as a young college student studying abroad in the Spanish city of Segovia. The family I stayed with took me out to the countryside to experience rural life, and we made paella over a fire. I still have the notes I jotted down 20 years ago. In Spanish, I wrote, "Never cook the rice more than 20 minutes." With sage advice like that, you'll have great paella, too.*

*You can put whatever you like in the paella, though it's common to see pork chorizo included in some parts of Spain. I've included my own Beef Chorizo in this recipe. It's best to use an extra-large paella pan to make this recipe, but if you don't have one, a big cazuela or Dutch oven will do.*

¼ cup olive oil

1 pound boneless skinless chicken thighs, cut into bite-size pieces

1 pound mixed seafood (calamari, shrimp, and mussels, for example), fresh or frozen

1 cup diced yellow onion

4–5 bay leaves

2 tablespoons *Achiote* Seasoning (see recipe on p. 170)

2 tablespoons smoked paprika

1½ tablespoons minced garlic

1 tablespoon tomato paste

2 teaspoons sea salt

¼ teaspoon freshly ground black pepper

1½ quarts Chicken Broth (see recipe on p. 32)

2 cups Arborio rice

2 cups fresh or frozen peas

1 cup thickly sliced Beef *Chorizo* (see recipe on p. 177)

Pinch saffron threads

1. In an extra-large paella pan or Dutch oven over medium–high heat, warm the oil. Add the chicken and sauté for 5 minutes, until brown on 1 side. Raise the heat to high, turn over the chicken, add the mixed seafood, and sauté for 5 minutes, until the chicken browns on the other side.

2. Add the onion, bay leaves, *Achiote* Seasoning, paprika, garlic, tomato paste, salt, and black pepper, and stir until well combined. Stir in the Chicken Broth and cook for 2 to 3 minutes.

3. Add the rice to the pan but do not mix or stir. Bring to a boil, reduce the heat to low, and add the peas, Beef *Chorizo*, and saffron. Cook, uncovered, for exactly 20 minutes. Remove from the heat.

4. Serve on individual plates or share with guests by having them surround the paella pan and serve themselves from it.

# Hibiscus Punch

*If you go into some Mexican markets here in the United States, you'll often find an area of the store that sells prepared Mexican favorites like tacos, tortas, and churros. You might also find some drinks there, like* tamarindo *(tamarind),* horchata *(rice) and* jamaica *(hibiscus). The hibiscus is my favorite because I truly love its smell and the flavor, but the most fun for me is cooking the flowers. Make it on a hot summer day. You can find dried hibiscus flowers in most Mexican markets around the country in the spice aisle.*

1½ quarts water

1 cup dried hibiscus flowers

1 cup honey

1 cup white grape juice (not from concentrate)

½ cup raw cane sugar

½ cup fresh lemon juice

1 In a large saucepan over medium–high heat, bring the water to a boil. Add the hibiscus flowers and cook for 3 to 5 minutes, until their color transfers to the water. Remove from the heat. Add the honey, grape juice, and sugar to the saucepan and stir until well combined.

2 Strain out and discard the flowers. Add the lemon juice and set aside to cool to room temperature.

3 Refrigerate for 4 to 6 hours.

4 Serve chilled over ice.

# No-Alcohol
# *Piña Colada*

*There's probably no other Latin drink that's more popular than the Piña Colada. The sweetness of the pineapple mixed in with silky coconut is delicious, but of course, the rum is not halal. I came up with a tasty alternative we've been making for friends for years. We particularly enjoy this when breaking the fast in Ramadan because it's so refreshing. For best results, use fresh, very ripe pineapple.*

3¾ cups fresh pineapple, diced

3 cups ice

1½ cups coconut cream

¼ cup + 2 tablespoons pineapple juice

4 pineapple chunks, for garnish (optional)

1  In a blender, combine the pineapple, ice, coconut cream, and pineapple juice. Purée for 1 minute, until thoroughly combined and mostly smooth.

2  If using, cut slits into each of the pineapple chunks and slide 1 on each serving glass. Divide the contents of the blender evenly among the 4 glasses and serve immediately.

YIELD: 6–8 SERVINGS

SPECIAL EQUIPMENT: 9-inch × 13-inch pan, 12¼-inch × ½-inch × 2¾-inch loaf pan, offset spatula or nonserrated knife, whisk

# Raspberry Flan

*This recipe is a bit of a twist on traditional flan, which has the same base flavors but no fruit on top.*

1¼ cups raw cane sugar, divided

¼ cup room-temperature water

1⅔ cups whole milk

1 cup heavy whipping cream

2 teaspoons Vanilla Extract (see recipe on p. 56) or 1 Bourbon vanilla bean pod, slit lengthwise

5 whole large eggs

2 egg yolks

1 quart boiling water

1 pound fresh or frozen raspberries

¼ cup granulated sugar

2 tablespoons fresh lemon juice

1   Preheat the oven to 325°F.

2   In a small saucepan over medium heat, combine 1 cup of the raw cane sugar and the room-temperature water and bring to a boil. Cook, lifting and swirling the pan to help the sugar dissolve, for 4 to 5 minutes, until the syrup turns a dark caramel color. Remove from the heat and immediately pour the syrup into a loaf pan.

3   In a medium saucepan over medium heat, combine the milk, cream, and Vanilla Extract (if using the vanilla bean, use the back of a nonserrated knife to scrape the seeds into the saucepan). While whisking vigorously as it cooks, slowly bring the mixture to a boil. Immediately remove from the heat and continue to whisk until the mixture thickens. Cover and set aside for 20 minutes.

4   In a large mixing bowl, combine the remaining ¼ cup raw cane sugar, eggs, and egg yolks and whisk vigorously for 2 to 3 minutes, until smooth and creamy. Slowly, in ½ cup increments, add the warmed milk–cream mixture to the mixing bowl while whisking constantly. Carefully transfer the custard to the syrup-lined dish, cover with foil, and set aside.

5   Place a 9-inch × 13-inch cake pan on the middle rack of the oven and pour the boiling water into it. Place the foil-covered loaf pan in the middle of the cake pan (the water in the cake pan should come up to about the same level as the custard in the loaf pan). Bake for 40 to 45 minutes, until a nonserrated knife inserted 2 inches from the edge of the flan comes out clean. Remove from the oven.

6   Loosen the flan from the loaf pan by sliding an offset spatula or nonserrated knife around the rim of the pan. Place a large platter over the loaf pan and quickly invert the pan; the flan should release onto the platter. Set aside to cool completely.

7   Refrigerate for 6 to 8 hours or overnight.

8   To make the syrup, in a medium saucepan over medium heat, combine the raspberries, granulated sugar, and lemon juice. Stir until well combined. Bring to a boil.

9   Reduce the heat to low and cook for 10 minutes. Remove from the heat and set aside to cool to room temperature.

10  Refrigerate the syrup overnight.

11  Serve the flan whole on the platter with the chilled syrup poured over it or slice the flan into long, thick pieces laid flat on dessert plates with the syrup drizzled on top.

YIELD: 1½ CUPS
SPECIAL EQUIPMENT: 1-quart glass storage container, whisk

# Dulce de Leche

*Dulce de Leche is the caramel of the Latin world. In Mexico, it's known as* cajeta *and traditionally made with goat's milk, but cow's milk is more common here in the United States. Like caramel, you can use this in all sorts of desserts, including cakes, candies, and ice creams.*

**3 cups whole milk**

**1½ cups raw cane sugar**

**½ teaspoon sea salt**

**½ teaspoon baking soda**

1  In a medium, deep-bottomed saucepan over medium heat, combine the milk and sugar and bring to a boil. Stir until the sugar is completely dissolved.

2  Reduce the heat to low and add the salt and baking soda to the saucepan, whisking until well combined.

3  Bring the mixture to a slow boil and then whisk vigorously, taking care to scrape down the sides of the pan. Raise the heat to medium–low and simmer for 2 hours, until the mixture takes on a darker, caramelized color.

4  Reduce the heat to low, whisk until completely smooth, and cook for 20 to 30 minutes but no longer. Remove from the heat.

5  Immediately transfer to a 1-quart glass storage container (otherwise it will harden and become very sticky). Set aside, uncovered, to cool to room temperature.

6  Cover the container and store in the refrigerator for up to 2 weeks.

YIELD: 1½ QUARTS

SPECIAL EQUIPMENT: Heat-safe glass bowl, ice cream machine, stainless 2-quart freezer-safe container with a lid, whisk

# *Dulce de Leche* Ice Cream

*If you love caramel-topped ice cream, this recipe will melt your heart. The* Dulce de Leche *is beautifully swirled into the ice cream. The peanuts are optional, but their salty contrast to the sweet* Dulce de Leche *is really delicious.*

**1 quart whole milk**

**2 cups whipping cream**

**2 teaspoons Vanilla Extract (see recipe on p. 56)**

**2 Bourbon vanilla bean pods, slit lengthwise**

**1½ cups *Dulce de Leche* (see recipe on p. 195), divided**

**Salted peanuts, optional**

1  In a medium saucepan over medium heat, combine the milk, cream, and Vanilla Extract. Using the back of a nonserrated knife, scrape the vanilla beans' seeds into the saucepan.

2  While whisking vigorously as it cooks, slowly bring the mixture almost to a boil. Immediately reduce the heat to medium–low and whisk ¾ cup of the *Dulce de Leche* into the mixture until it is fully incorporated. Quickly remove from the heat.

3  Transfer the contents of the saucepan to a heat-safe bowl and set aside to cool completely.

4  Cover the glass bowl with plastic wrap and refrigerate for 4 to 6 hours or overnight.

5  Transfer the contents of the glass bowl to the chilled bowl of an ice cream machine. Drizzle about ⅓ cup of the *Dulce de Leche* into the machine's bowl and churn for 20 minutes on low to medium speed, until the ice cream is thick and has a similar consistency to gelato.

6  Place ½ of the ice cream to a stainless 2-quart freezer-safe container. Drizzle the remaining *Dulce de Leche* over the top and, using a knife, swirl it into a pattern. Place the remaining ice cream on top of the swirled *Dulce de Leche*, cover, and freeze for at least 4 to 6 hours.

7  Let the ice cream sit at room temperature for 2 to 3 minutes before scooping. Serve in bowls with the salted peanuts, if using. Any remaining ice cream will store in the freezer for 2 to 3 weeks.

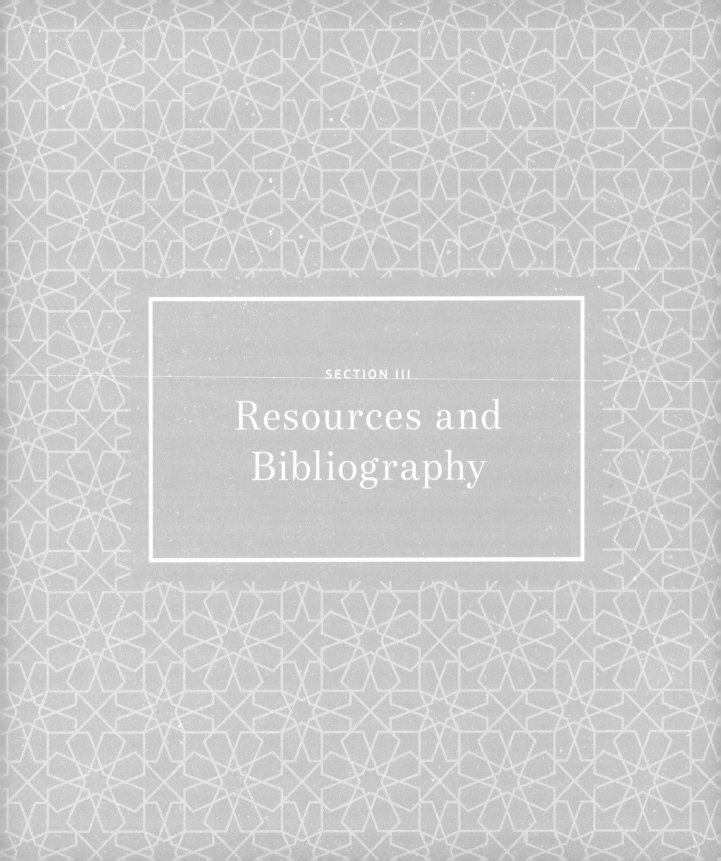

SECTION III

# Resources and Bibliography

# Resources for Halal Cooking and Baking

### ACTIVE DRY YEAST

Red Star Yeast

redstaryeast.com

### BAKING SPECIALTY ITEMS

Edible sugar pearls: Wilton

wilton.com

### CHEESE AND DAIRY PRODUCTS

Cabot Creamery

cabotcheese.coop

Kerrygold butter

kerrygoldusa.com

Organic vegetable rennet for cheesemaking: New England Cheesemaking Supply Company

cheesemaking.com

Organic Valley cheese and milk

organicvalley.coop

Tillamook

tillamook.com

### CHOCOLATE PRODUCTS

Chocolat Uzma Sharif

chocolatuzma.com

Dutch cocoa products: Frontier Fair Trade Cocoa Powder, Certified Organic

Godiva (some varieties are certified halal)

godiva.com

Single-origin roasted cocoa nibs: Askinosie Chocolate

askinosie.com

### COCONUT PRODUCTS

Chaokoh Coconut Milk (found in most Asian grocers and international supermarkets)

### COFFEE

Café Bustelo

cafebustelo.com

Lavazza

lavazza.com

### CONDIMENTS AND SPREADS

Trader Joe's Creamy and Unsalted Peanut Butter: Trader Joe's stores

### SPECIALTY COOKWARE

Carbon steel paella pan

paellapans.com

Paella pan by Garcima (made in Spain): World Market stores and from Garcima
garcima.com/productos/paellas

## DARK GLASS BOTTLES AND JARS

Beanilla Trading Company
beanilla.com/glass-bottles-jars

## FISH AND SEAFOOD

Maine Whole Cherrystone Clams: Trader Joe's stores

## FLOUR

King Arthur All-Purpose Flour
kingarthurflour.com

Ceresota flour
heckersceresota.com

## GELATIN AND FOOD-GRADE GLYCERIN

Hoosier Hill Farm Agar Agar Powder
hoosierhillfarm.com

NOW Solutions Vegetable Glycerin (an all-natural product derived from non-GMO palm or vegetable oil): Whole Foods Market stores and NOW Foods
nowfoods.com

NOW Real Food Agar Powder (derived entirely from seaweed; a product of Morocco): NOW Foods
nowfoods.com

The Seaweed Solution Excellent Gel Strength Agar Agar Powder (vegan and gluten-free)
amazon.com

## HALAL CERTIFICATION BODIES

Halal Food Standards Alliance of America
halaladvocates.net/site/hfsaa/about-hfsaa

Islamic Food and Nutrition Council of America
ifanca.org

Islamic Services of America
isahalal.org

Shar'I Zabiha Certification of Rahmat E-Alam Foundation
rahmatealam.net

## ITALIAN SPECIALTY ITEMS

Forno Bonomi Ladyfingers
fornobonomi.com

Trader Joe's Soft Lady Fingers: Trader Joe's stores

## JUICES

Trader Joe's Certified Organic Pasteurized Concord Grape Juice (100% juice): Trader Joe's stores

Trader Joe's Certified Organic Pasteurized 100% Pomegranate Juice (100% juice from organic concentrate): Trader Joe's stores

Trader Joe's Certified Organic Pasteurized White Grape Juice (100% juice from organic concentrate): Trader Joe's stores

## MARSHMALLOWS

Halal marshmallows made to order: Chocolat Uzma Sharif
chocolatuzma.com

Dandies Air Puffed Marshmallows (vegan, gluten-free, gelatin-free, and GMO-free marshmallows)
veganstore.com or halalville.com

Ziyad Brand Halal Marshmallows (available at most Middle Eastern and Mediterranean markets)
eyelevellink.com

## MASA FOR TAMALES

La Guadalupana Masa Natural
senortamale.com

## MEATS AND SAUSAGE CASINGS

Barkaat Foods
barkaatfoods.com

Crescent Foods
crescenthalal.com

Halal Pastures (organic, halal, grass-fed, hormone and antibiotic-free meat and farm products)
halalpastures.com

Holy Cow Organic Halal Meats (organic halal meat and poultry products from Michigan farmers)
holyhalalcow.com

Jenna Foods
jennafoods.com

Midamar Halal
midamarhalal.com

Nema Food Company (also found in many Mediterranean and Middle Eastern stores)
nemahalal.com

Saffron Road Food
saffronroadfood.com

## MOLASSES

Golden Barrel Unsulfured Blackstrap Molasses
goldenbarrel.com

Grandma's Robust Unsulphured Molasses
grandmasmolasses.com

## OILS

House of Tsang Pure Sesame Oil
houseoftsang.com

Kadoya Pure Sesame Oil
amazon.com

Trader Joe's Toasted Sesame Oil: Trader Joe's stores

## PASTRY BRUSHES

Koromiko pastry brushes (made of birch and horse hair)
koromiko.com

Mjölk Pastry Brush
store.mjolk.ca

OXO Good Grips Silicone basting and pastry brushes
oxo.com

## SAUCES AND SYRUPS

Monin flavored sauces and syrups
moninstore.com

Trader Joe's Fleur de Sel Caramel Sauce: Trader Joe's stores

## SAUSAGE-MAKING SUPPLIES

Beef or lamb casings: check with your local halal meat market or butcher or Sara Meat Market, 9001 N. Milwaukee Avenue, Niles, IL 60714, 847-581-0792

KitchenAid Mixer Sausage Stuffer Kit
kitchenaid.com/shop

## SPICES

Mountain Rose Herbs organic herbs and spices
mountainroseherbs.com

Penzeys Spices
penzeys.com

## TAPIOCA PEARLS

Tapioca Pearl by Golden Country Oriental Food Co., Chicago, IL 60608

## TOFU

Ichiban Soft Tofu

## VANILLA BEANS

Vanilla Products USA Madagascar Bourbon Vanilla Beans 6-7"
vanillaproductsusa.com

## VINEGAR PRODUCTS

Bragg's Organic Apple Cider Vinegar
bragg.com

Date Vinegar
datevinegar.com

# Bibliography

al-Jawziyya, Ibn Qayyim. *Medicine of the Prophet.* Translated by Penelope Johnstone. 1998. Cambridge: The Islamic Texts Society, 1998.

al-Qasim, Abdul Malik. *Eating Etiquette According to the Quran, the Sunnah, and the Pious Predecessors.* Translated by Muhammad Abdul Majeed Ahmad. Kerala: International Islamic Publishing House, 1999.

Fallon, Sally and Mary Enig. *Nourishing Traditions: The Cookbook that Challenges Politically Correct Nutrition and the Diet Dictocrats.* Rev. 2nd ed. White Plains, Maryland: New Trends Publishing, 2001.

Fallon, Sally. "Broth Is Beautiful." *Weston A. Price Foundation for Wise Traditions.* January 1, 2000. http://www.westonaprice.org/health-topics/broth-is-beautiful/

Galarza, Daniela. "The Bone Broth Trend Isn't Going Anywhere: Here's What You Need to Know." *Eater.com.* February 12, 2015. http://www.eater.com/2015/2/12/8025027/what-is-bone-broth-and-why-is-everyone-talking-about-it

Joachim, David. *The Food Substitutions Bible: More than 6,500 Substitutions for Ingredients, Equipment & Techniques.* 2nd ed. Toronto: Robert Rose, 2010.

Mercola, Dr. Joseph. "Bone Broth: One of Your Most Healing Diet Staples." *Mercola.com.* Dec. 16, 2013. http://articles.mercola.com/sites/articles/archive/2013/12/16/bone-broth-benefits.aspx

Qadhi, Shaykh Yasir. *Precious Provisions:* Fiqh *of Food and Clothing.* Class, AlMaghrib Institute.

Sakr, Dr. Ahmad H., Ph.D. *Gelatin.* Walnut: Foundation for Islamic Knowledge, 1999.

Tayo, Abolade Nkosi. *Pork Eating: The Great Risk to Human Health.* New Delhi: Islamic Book Service, 2004.

Weston, Nicole. "What is Bourbon Vanilla?" *BakingBites.com.* June 5, 2012. http://bakingbites.com/2012/06/what-is-bourbon-vanilla/

Zaouali, Lilia. *Medieval Cuisine of the Islamic World: A Concise History with 174 Recipes.* Translated by M.B. DeBevoise. American ed. Berkeley: University of California Press, 2007.

# Acknowledgments

THIS BOOK WAS A LABOR OF LOVE INSPIRED FROM ABOVE. Without the help and guidance of Allah (God), none of it could have been possible or remotely feasible. All the good in this work comes from Him, and any shortcomings are from me alone. *Alhamdullilah*, all thanks and praises are due to Him alone for blessing me with the honor and responsibility of carrying this work through to the end.

I'd also like to thank Agate Publishing, and particularly its founder, Doug Seibold, for taking on this project, at a time when information relating to Islam is grossly misconstrued. They are visionaries who helped facilitate my dream of bringing halal cuisine to tables around the world through this book.

Thanks to my agent, Sally Ekus, who believed enough in the timeliness and significance of my work to connect me with Doug and his team of professionals at Agate Publishing. She has been a kind and gentle mentor in my first foray into the traditional publishing world.

My heartfelt thanks go out to author and my book coach, Dianne Jacob. Without her help over the past several years, I'm not sure where this book would be today. She was instrumental in providing the guidance necessary to get the outline of this book on paper, and helped me believe it was a book that needed to be published.

I could never give enough thanks to my mom, for all she has done to help me realize my dream of writing this book. She gave me everything from my first subscription to *Martha Stewart Living* to the best kitchen tools a cook could ask for—only she knew what was really in my heart to pursue. I love you, Mom.

I thank my dad, who gave me my first camera when I was a young girl and encouraged me to take pictures of the beautiful meals on our table. He helped me recognize beauty everywhere, including the glorious art of creating a meal. I love you, Dad.

I thank both of my late grandmothers, whom sadly will not have a chance to see this book. They will never know how much I admired the way they lovingly fed the people in their lives and the inspiration I continue to draw from their lives. Thank you, Nonna and Abuela. I love you both.

I thank Carlos for suggesting I write down my recipes for the world to see, and for setting me on a journey that gave me the strength necessary to pull it all together.

Without the support of my family and friends, it would have been much more challenging to work on this book. In addition to my extended family, heartfelt thanks go to my dear friends—Inci Kirman, Rosanna Granata, Noor Church, Sue Labadi, and Arshia Ali-Khan—for standing by me, believing in me, and sacrificing time to always be there for me.

Thanks go to my assistant Yemeen Shamsi, who dedicated long days and nights to recipe testing. It wouldn't have been nearly as much fun without her.

Thanks go to the Echevarria family at Dream Kitchen in Elgin, Illinois, for providing a great commercial kitchen space for recipe testing, and also incredibly helpful feedback on my dishes.

Last, but certainly not least, I thank the Islamic Food and Nutrition Council of America (IFANCA), for answering many of my questions on food science; Rachid Belbachir, for explaining halal from a variety of Islamic sources; Catherine Lambrecht, of the Culinary Historians of Chicago, for inviting me to present about halal food; Hanan Ahmed, for volunteering her photography skills; and my blogger friends, Asma Khan, Catherine Macera, and Kareema Falih, who meticulously tested recipes and provided feedback.

# Index

*Note:* Italic page numbers indicate photos.

# About the Author

YVONNE MAFFEI, MA, is a graduate of Ohio University (Spanish, Latin American, and International Studies). She is passionate about home cooking, global cuisine, organic gardening, world travel, and learning about other cultures. She aims to teach others about these subjects on her website, MyHalalKitchen.com; through her workshops, lectures, and cooking demos; and with this book.

Yvonne is a native of Amherst, Ohio, but today lives near Chicago, where she is pursuing the creation of a working organic farm.

# Metric Conversions

## VOLUME CONVERSIONS

| U.S. | METRIC |
|---|---|
| 1 teaspoon | 5 milliliters |
| 1 tablespoon | 15 milliliters |
| ¼ cup | 59 milliliters |
| ⅓ cup | 79 milliliters |
| ½ cup | 118 milliliters |
| ⅔ cup | 158 milliliters |
| ¾ cup | 177 milliliters |
| 1 cup | 237 milliliters |
| 2 cups | 473 milliliters |
| 3 cups | 710 milliliters |
| 4 cups (1 quart) | 946 milliliters |
| 1.06 quarts | 1 liter |
| 4 quarts (1 gallon) | 3.8 liters |

## WEIGHT CONVERSIONS

| U.S. | METRIC |
|---|---|
| ½ ounce | 14 grams |
| ¾ ounce | 21 grams |
| 1 ounce | 28 grams |
| 1½ ounces | 43 grams |
| 2 ounces | 57 grams |
| 2½ ounces | 71 grams |
| 3 ounces | 85 grams |
| 4 ounces | 113 grams |
| 5 ounces | 142 grams |
| 6 ounces | 170 grams |
| 7 ounces | 198 grams |
| 8 ounces | 227 grams |
| 9 ounces | 255 grams |
| 10 ounces | 284 grams |
| 12 ounces | 340 grams |
| 16 ounces (1 pound) | 454 grams |
| 2.2 pounds | 1 kilogram |

## OVEN TEMPERATURES

| FAHRENHEIT | CELSIUS |
|---|---|
| 225 | 110 |
| 250 | 120 |
| 275 | 140 |
| 300 | 150 |
| 325 | 160 |
| 350 | 180 |
| 375 | 190 |
| 400 | 200 |
| 425 | 220 |
| 450 | 230 |
| 475 | 250 |
| 500 | 260 |